PAPAL GUIDANCE ON TEACHING THE FAITH

PAPAL GUIDANCE ON TEACHING THE FAITH

12 TIMELESS DOCUMENTS ON THE PRESERVATION OF DOCTRINE

Arranged & Introduced by

BISHOP ATHANASIUS SCHNEIDER

SOPHIA INSTITUTE PRESS
MANCHESTER, NEW HAMPSHIRE

First published in the USA
by Sophia Institute Press

All magisterial documents are here reproduced from previously approved English translations from the public domain or with permission of the original publisher, excepting Bishop Schneider's original translations of *Etsi Minime* and *Orbem Catholicum*. See Acknowledgments for complete references.

Scripture quotations are either translator originals from the Latin Vulgate, or drawn from the Challoner version of the Douay-Rheims Bible per the imprint of John Murphy Company (Baltimore, 1899). Citations are given in accord with the latter.

Cover design by Enrique J. Aguilar
Front cover art: Saint Gregory the Great, Pope by
Francisco de Goya (Wikimedia Commons)

Sophia Institute Press
Box 5284, Manchester, NH 03108
1-800-888-9344

www.SophiaInstitute.com

ISBN 979-8-88911-600-4
eBook ISBN 979-8-88911-601-1
Library of Congress Control Number: 2025945408

First printing

CONTENTS

SCRIPTURE CITATION ABBREVIATIONS

Abbr	Douay-Rheims	Contemporary
1 Cor	1 Corinthians	1 Corinthians
1 Esd	1 Esdras	Ezra
1 Jn	1 John	1 John
1 Kgs	1 Kings	1 Samuel
1 Mc	1 Machabees	1 Maccabees
1 Par	1 Paralipomenon	1 Chronicles
1 Pt	1 Peter	1 Peter
1 Thes	1 Thessalonians	1 Thessalonians
1 Tm	1 Timothy	1 Timothy
2 Cor	2 Corinthians	2 Corinthians
2 Esd	2 Esdras	Nehemiah
2 Jn	2 John	2 John
2 Kgs	2 Kings	2 Samuel
2 Mc	2 Machabees	2 Maccabees
2 Par	2 Paralipomenon	2 Chronicles
2 Pt	2 Peter	2 Peter
2 Thes	2 Thessalonians	2 Thessalonians
2 Tm	2 Timothy	2 Timothy
3 Jn	3 John	3 John
3 Kgs	3 Kings	1 Kings
4 Kgs	4 Kings	2 Kings
Abd	Abdias	Obadiah
Acts	Acts of the Apostles	Acts of the Apostles
Agg	Aggeus	Haggai
Am	Amos	Amos
Apoc	Apocalypse	Revelation
Bar	Baruch	Baruch
Cant	Canticle of Canticles	Song of Songs
Col	Colossians	Colossians
Dn	Daniel	Daniel
Dt	Deuteronomy	Deuteronomy
Eccles	Ecclesiastes	Ecclesiastes
Ecclus	Ecclesiasticus	Sirach
Eph	Ephesians	Ephesians
Est	Esther	Esther
Ex	Exodus	Exodus
Ez	Ezechiel	Ezekiel
Gal	Galatians	Galatians
Gn	Genesis	Genesis
Hb	Habacuc	Habbakuk
Heb	Hebrews	Hebrews
Is	Isaias	Isaiah
Jas	James	James
Jer	Jeremias	Jeremiah
Jb	Job	Job
Jl	Joel	Joel
Jn	John	John
Jon	Jonas	Jonas
Jo	Josue	Joshua
Jude	Jude	Jude
Jgs	Judges	Judges
Jdt	Judith	Judith
Lam	Lamentations	Lamentations
Lv	Leviticus	Leviticus
Lk	Luke	Luke
Mal	Malachias	Malachi
Mk	Mark	Mark
Mt	Matthew	Matthew
Mi	Micheas	Micah
Na	Nahum	Nahum
Nm	Numbers	Numbers
Os	Osee	Hosea
Phlm	Philemon	Philemon
Phil	Philippians	Philippians
Prv	Proverbs	Proverbs
Ps	Psalms	Psalms
Rom	Romans	Romans
Ru	Ruth	Ruth
Soph	Sophonias	Zephaniah
Ti	Titus	Titus
Tb	Tobias	Tobit
Ws	Wisdom	Wisdom
Zac	Zacharias	Zechariah

"For there shall be a time, when they will not endure
sound doctrine;... and will indeed turn away their
hearing from the truth, but will be turned unto fables."

(2 Timothy 4:3–4)

ACKNOWLEDGMENTS

In the preparation of this work for English publication, I am again indebted to Mr. Charlie McKinney and the other remarkable men and women of Sophia Institute Press, as well as Mr. Aaron Seng and his Tradivox research team, who have been so helpful in locating some of the authorized English translations of the documents compiled herein.

The sources of the magisterial texts included in this book are as follows:

Etsi Minime. English translation by Bishop Athanasius Schneider from the original Italian at Libreria Editrice Vaticana, accessed January 1, 2025, https://www.vatican.va/content/benedictus-xiv/it/documents/enciclica--i-etsi-minime--i---7-febbraio-1742--affermata-la-prim.html.

Cum Religiosi. English translation authorized by Bishop F. Joseph Gossman, reproduced with permission of the publisher from Sr. Claudia Carlen, IHM, ed., *The Papal Encyclicals: 1740–1878* (The Pierian Press, 1990).

In Dominico Agro. English translation authorized by Bishop F. Joseph Gossman, reproduced with permission of the publisher from Sr. Claudia Carlen, IHM, ed., *The Papal Encyclicals: 1740–1878* (The Pierian Press, 1990).

Probe Nostis. English translation authorized by Bishop F. Joseph Gossman, reproduced with permission of the publisher from

Sr. Claudia Carlen, IHM, ed., *The Papal Encyclicals: 1740–1878* (The Pierian Press, 1990).

Quanta Cura. English translation from *The Year of Preparation for the Vatican Council: Including the Original and English of the Encyclical and Syllabus, and of the Papal Documents Connected with Its Convocation*, ed. Rev. Herbert Vaughan, (Burns, Oates, and Company, 1869), existing in the public domain. The text of the Syllabus of Errors appended to *Quanta Cura* is from the more readable version authorized by Paul Cardinal Cullen in *The Syllabus for the People: A Review of the Propositions Condemned by His Holiness Pope Pius IX with Text of the Condemned List*, translated by a monk of St. Augustine's (The Catholic Publication Society, 1875), also found in the public domain.

Spectata Fides. English translation authorized by Bishop F. Joseph Gossman, reproduced with permission of the publisher from Sr. Claudia Carlen IHM, ed., *The Papal Encyclicals: 1878–1903* (The Pierian Press, 1990).

Acerbo Nimis. English translation authorized by Bishop F. Joseph Gossman, reproduced with permission of the publisher from Sr. Claudia Carlen IHM, ed., *The Papal Encyclicals: 1903–1939* (The Pierian Press, 1990).

Lamentabili Sane. English translation authorized by Bishop Peter Bartholome, from *All Things in Christ: Encyclical Letters and Selected Documents of Saint Pius X*, trans. Rev. Vincent A. Yzermans (The Newman Press, 1954), found in the public domain.

Sacrorum Antistitum. English translated anonymously from *The American Catholic Quarterly Review*35, no. 140 (1910): 712–731, found in the public domain.

Orbem Catholicum. English translation by Bishop Athanasius Schneider from the original Latin at Libreria Editrice Vaticana, accessed January 1, 2025, https://www.vatican.va/content/pius-xi/

la/motu_proprio/documents/hf_p-xi_motu-proprio_19230629_orbem-catholicum.html.

Divini Illius Magistri. English translation reproduced with permission from Papal Encyclicals Online, accessed March 19, 2025 at https://www.papalencyclicals.net/pius11/p11rappr.htm.

Provido Sane Consilium. English translation authorized by Patrick Cardinal Hayes, from *A Handbook of the Confraternity of Christian Doctrine*, ed. Rev. John S. Middleton (Benziger Brothers, 1937), found in the public domain.

Call for Capable Catechists. Taken from *A Handbook of the Confraternity of Christian Doctrine*, ed. Rev. John S. Middleton (Benziger Brothers, 1937), found in the public domain.

PAPAL GUIDANCE ON TEACHING THE FAITH

Introduction

WHY THIS BOOK?

When diagnosing the evils of the early twentieth century, Pope St. Pius X declared that the greatest misfortune and disaster was "ignorance of divine things."[1]

A century later, we look around to see a social and cultural landscape that appears barely recognizable as the same world of the early 1900s. We have witnessed the fragmentation of nearly all social relations into disembodied, digitally-delivered clouds of information often saturated with advertisement and consumerism; the breakdown of the nuclear family and its replacement with all manner of unnatural "unions"; the destruction of local and national identities, autonomy, self-governance, and security in the name of greater "tolerance"; the legalized and nationally-subsidized murder of the unborn and the inconvenient; the barbaric harvest and sale of fetal stem cells on the international market; and a host of other social evils that become almost unnamable.

While the remedy to all such evil is and has always been the integral knowledge and practice of right doctrine—that which has been revealed by God and retained in the Catholic Church alone—we are now alarmed to observe that those who ought to hold and propagate this remedy are too often found negligent in proclaiming it, if not apparently ignorant of this doctrine in the first place. Suffice it to cite the last several years of religious surveys in the United States, where millions of self-identifying Catholics apparently do not know even the most basic tenets of their religion, and still less often practice its moral precepts.[2] This pattern now recurs throughout the

1 Encyclical *Acerbo Nimis* (April 15, 1905), no. 1.

2 See, for example, the findings of the Pew Research Surveys published in 2024 and 2025.

world as the bitter fruit of what Pope Benedict XVI identified in the 1990s as "the catastrophic failure of modern catechesis."[3]

If there is to be any hope of authentic restoration in the art of teaching the Faith today, a number of basic questions must first be answered: What is this Faith, and how do we know it with certainty? What is catechesis, and how should it be practiced? To answer these questions and others of similar kind, a return to basic truths is necessary.

Such a "return to basics" in Catholic catechesis has been my chief motivation in preparing this text. After Our Lord and His holy saints, there are few better teachers in this regard than the holy popes of the previous century; so marked for their pastoral zeal and intellectual vigor, and who taught during a period of global change and challenge not so different from our own, calling for renewed attention to the art and discipline of catechesis. In this *Papal Guidance on Teaching the Faith*, I have sought to gather their most important instructions on the matter, offering them in a clear English translation for the benefit especially of Catholic teachers and students, whether clerics or laypersons. This marks the first time that these documents have ever appeared together in print, and I trust they will serve as a helpful reference for the future.

I enjoin readers to give particular attention to the texts included from the great "Pope of the Catechism," Pope St. Pius X (reigned 1903–1914). Although perhaps better known for changing the required age for receiving Holy Communion in the Roman Rite, this holy pontiff may be most honored for his emphasis on sound doctrine, effective teaching methods, and stalwart opposition to errors in matters of faith and morals during his pontificate. As he rose to meet the challenge of a rapidly growing infiltration of Modernist theology[4] into Catholic schools and seminaries, several

3 *The Yes of Jesus Christ* (Crossroad Publishing Company, 1991), 35.

4 For a concise treatment of the Modernist heresy and other doctrinal errors faced by the Church throughout the centuries, I recommend my work, *Flee from Heresy: A Catholic Guide to Ancient and Modern Errors* (Sophia Institute Press, 2024).

documents from his teaching magisterium discuss instruction on authentic Catholic doctrine as a check to the various errors of the period: errors that would reemerge with great force some fifty years later and continue to plague many institutions of the Church in our own time.

The instructions of Pius X in matters of doctrine may therefore be regarded as a kind of recapitulation of the Church's perennial catechetical praxis, and a prime characterization of the true *shepherd of souls*: one who feeds and guides the sheep, defending them from the errors of false doctrine and its teachers, already foreseen as "ravening wolves" in the ranks of the Catholic hierarchy by St. Paul (see Acts 20:29). Those involved in preaching and teaching today will therefore do well to make especially careful study of this holy pontiff's observations.

The editorial changes made to the documents collected here have been very few, but merit some description. First, all annotations have been standardized, with Scripture citations appearing in-text and all other references being moved to footnotes. A few citations have been added or expanded for convenience; e.g., among the many Scriptural allusions made in the documents, some of these have also been cited where it seemed suitable. Paragraph breaks and numbering have been added or adjusted so that these English translations match those found in the Vatican Library. As such, paragraph numbering now appears in every document, allowing for easier navigation when compared against the magisterial base texts. Section subtitles have also been included—either retained from approved English editions or newly added for this publication—so that the content and arrangement of the material will stand out more clearly.

Finally, inasmuch as the Latin Vulgate remains the most venerable and canonically approved translation of Scripture to be utilized in the official acts of the Church, the Biblical text citations throughout this work have been sourced from Bishop Challoner's approved rendition of the Douay-Rheims English rendering of the

Clementine Vulgate, as found in John Murphy Company's edition of 1899. For readers less familiar with this edition of the Bible or its more abbreviated reference system, a citations table has been included to facilitate greater understanding (see p. vii).

It is my hope that everyone who reads this book seeking to better know and hand on the true Faith will find instruction and nourishment in these pages. As "love follows knowledge,"[5] may you, my dear reader, both grow in knowledge and lead others to the same, as St. Augustine exhorts: "Instruct in such a manner that he to whom you are discoursing upon hearing may believe, in believing may hope, and in hoping may love."[6] May the Blessed Virgin Mary, Queen of Heaven and earth, intercede for you and for all who undertake this most necessary task today.

May 31, 2025, Feast of the Queenship of the Blessed Virgin Mary
✠ *Athanasius Schneider, Auxiliary Bishop of the Archdiocese of Saint Mary in Astana*

5 St. Thomas Aquinas, *Summa Theologiae* [ST], II-II, q. 27, a. 3, obj. 2.
6 *De catechizandis rudibus*, chap. 4.

Etsi Minime

ENCYCLICAL ON INSTRUCTION OF THE FAITHFUL

Pope Benedict XIV

February 7, 1742

To the Venerable Brothers, Patriarchs, Primates, Archbishops, and Bishops. Venerable Brothers, Greetings and Apostolic Blessing.

Although we hold no doubt that all those to whom the care of souls has been entrusted—and you above all, Venerable Brothers, elevated to the office of the apostolate and constituted by God in the dignity of the prelature and directing your foremost concern to ensure that the Christian people, nourished in a salutary way with the rudiments of the Faith and the pasture of heavenly doctrine, are happily guided along the path of the Lord's precepts under your luminous example—We cannot refrain from encouraging you, with the exhortations of Our authority and paternal love, to promote with greater solicitude the sacrosanct and salutary work of Christian doctrine, eliminating the harmful obstacles that hinder the salvation of souls.

Clear Understanding Is Necessary

1. Since We address persons well-versed in the law and exhort prudent bishops of the churches, who lack neither piety nor the resources of Sacred Scriptures, We deem it superfluous to repeat with extensive arguments that it is insufficient, for attaining heavenly happiness, to believe vaguely and indistinctly the mysteries revealed by God and taught by the Catholic Church.

This heavenly doctrine, transmitted by God and received through hearing (see Rom 10:14–17), must be received from the voice of a legitimate and faithful teacher, in such a way that its fundamental truths are individually explained and proposed to the faithful as truths to believe, some out of necessity of means, others out of necessity for precept.

Even though We affirm that justification is obtained through faith, as it is the principle and foundation of salvation leading ultimately to the desired lasting city, it is equally clear that faith alone is not sufficient (see Jas 2:26). One must both know and constantly remain on the path, that is, the precepts of God and the Church, the virtues to be cultivated and the vices to be carefully avoided.

Catechesis, the Task of Bishops

2. Since all this is contained in the first rudiments of the Catholic Faith or Christian doctrine as it is commonly called, it is the specific task of the bishops that this is illustrated in all the dioceses and in every place in a clear and methodical way; and they cannot neglect it without tacitly condemning themselves in conscience. Rather, they must devote all their care and diligence to this supremely necessary work.

We do not assert that this duty is so exclusively assigned to the bishop as to require his constant presence in teaching Christian doctrine, personally interrogating children and explaining the mysteries of the Faith we profess. We know very well the heavy burdens imposed by the apostolic ministry upon pastoral care. Our own experience in governing, first the Church of Ancona, and later that of Bologna taught Us how a prelate who strives to fulfill his duties entirely is beset by endless and diverse concerns like the waves of the sea.

This task will be carried out by the bishop who, even at times other than that of the pastoral visit, will sometimes be present where sound doctrine is transmitted to the Christian, questioning boys and girls about what they have learned, and explaining with his own words the mysteries of our religion. Such pastoral involvement will be greatly beneficial to the flock entrusted to him, and his example will encourage others to labor zealously in the vineyard of the Lord of hosts.

3. This manner of caring for the Church was defined almost as a law, not only by ancient but also by more recent prelates included in the roll of the blessed, such as Charles Borromeo, Francis de Sales, Turibius, and Alexander Sauli. Some of them, as their writings attest, when hindered by greater tasks, assigned this grave duty to a vicar chosen from among the canons or priests, who would take on this pastoral ministry to educate the young in the fundamental truths of the Faith and the duties of religion.

4. Therefore, the bishop's example, as mentioned above, will be of immense importance and great utility for the spiritual growth of souls if he carries out this duty in all parishes, at all times, and especially during his visits throughout the diocese.

However, as anyone can imagine, his strength alone will not suffice. To achieve the desired goal, it is necessary that he diligently ensures those he selects as vicars are imbued with zeal and concern in this praiseworthy and meritorious work.

Catechesis, the Duty of Pastors

5. First of all, there are two imposed by the Council of Trent on those who have the care of souls.[7] The first is to deliver sermons on divine matters on feast days. The second is to teach the rudiments of the Faith to children and anyone ignorant of the divine law.

If, on the appointed days, parish priests deliver the required homily—one that does not burden the ears with persuasive words of human wisdom but instills the Spirit in the hearts of listeners through words suited to their understanding; if they proclaim a

[7] See Session 5, *Decree on Reformation*, chap. 2; Session 22, *Doctrine on the Sacrifice of the Mass*, chap. 8; and Session 24, *Decree on Reformation*, chaps. 4, 7.

mystery, particularly during the season when the Church commemorates it, sowing what incites virtue and rejects vices, especially the gravest ones that most shamefully plague the people; if on these same days, they nurture children, as if newborns, with the milk of doctrine, questioning them individually, resolving doubts, and clarifying uncertainties; if finally, as the apostle directs, they devote themselves to reading, exhortation, and teaching so that the believer may become perfect and prepared for every good work (see 2 Tm 3:14–17)—then it is permissible to hope that the results will meet expectations and that a people pleasing to God and zealous for good works will easily emerge.

Others Assist in Catechesis

6. It is also amply shown throughout history that the labor of the parish priest alone is insufficient, since one cannot teach everyone when the number of the faithful surpasses the capacity of the teacher. Yet the bishop who devotes his heart and zeal to the welfare of the Church entrusted to him will never be without adequate remedies. He will be able to appeal to those who are approaching the tonsure, to those who are approaching the dignity of the priesthood by climbing the steps of the minor and major orders, and to those who, finally, are working to find a way to secure ecclesiastical benefits. The bishop will remind them, with authoritative and harsh words (and let deeds correspond to words), that he will never consent to the tonsure, once the proper age has been reached, or to the conferral of minor orders, but especially of major orders, of those who have neglected to assure the parish priests of their availability to teach Christian doctrine.

The bishop should assign these clerics to individual parishes in his city and diocese, designating some to specific churches. Moreover, he should make it known, with assurances, that diligence and zeal in this work will weigh significantly in the granting of parishes and other benefices by the law. This will ensure it is evident that the task of teaching is not the exclusive responsibility of the diocesan head but that many must collaborate to accomplish his mandate.

7. To all this, together with the sacred apostolic constitutions and particularly with the seventh of Leo X, Our predecessor of happy memory, it must be added that appropriate provisions have been established to ensure that schoolmasters, in teaching their pupils, and pious women, in instructing young girls (under the earnest exhortation of the bishop), nourish and strengthen them with sound and pure doctrine, as though it were vital nourishment.

It is also well established that the bishop himself can and must firmly encourage sacred preachers to instill in the ears and minds of parents, during sermons, the importance of instructing their children in the truths of our religion. Should the parents be unable to fulfill this duty, it will be necessary to bring the children to church, where the precepts of the divine law are explained.

In many places (and where it does not yet exist, it should be introduced), the pious and praiseworthy custom has also taken root of laypersons—both men and women—offering assistance to the parish priest in fulfilling this task. These lay assistants dedicate themselves to Christian instruction by listening to children and young girls recite from memory the Our Father, the Angelic Salutation, the Apostles' Creed, and all other prayers.

In other places, congregations have been established for the purpose of teaching Christian doctrine, an institution rightfully praised by Pius V of holy memory in his Constitution beginning with *Ex debito*.[8] He urged that these congregations be promoted with all diligence in every diocese.

If all these measures directed toward the same purpose are carefully cultivated, they will provide everyone with the assured certainty that, although the laborers are few where the harvest is

[8] Brief *Ex debito pastoralis officii* (July 2, 1571).

abundant, there will be no lack of those who will break the bread for the children who implore it (see Mt 9:37; and Lam 4:4).

8. It is also well known that not only children and those of more mature years lie in ignorance of divine matters, but also men and even the elderly are often found to be quite unaware of the saving doctrine, either because they never learned it or because, having once acquired it long ago, forgetfulness has gradually erased it. This ailment, too, can be remedied by the provident diligence of bishops if their collaborators take care to employ the remedies provided with proper attention.

Education of Children

9. Turning our attention to those in early childhood, many seek admission to the Holy Eucharist and confirmation. Indeed, few fail to show a strong will for this, as though driven by an irresistible desire. Therefore, the bishop should admonish parish priests and firmly command them not to admit to the Sacrament of the Eucharist, nor to issue the so-called confirmation card, to anyone who does not know the fundamentals of the Faith and doctrine, as well as the value and efficacy of the Sacrament. In this way, the needs of early childhood may be well addressed.

10. As for adolescents, since each one receives their own gift from God, experience clearly shows that some pursue the path of ecclesiastical life, while others follow that of secular life.

    Concerning the former, we have already addressed them when speaking of those who desire to be admitted to holy orders. It seems only one additional point may be made: it would be fitting and highly beneficial for the prelate, when examining candidates, to first inquire into the core substance of Christian knowledge. For experience, the teacher of truth has clearly shown that some candidates, though adorned with elegant and refined Latin eloquence, well-versed in a multitude of sciences, and possessing a thorough knowledge of all matters pertaining to the orders, have responded unsatisfactorily and irrelevantly when questioned on Christian doctrine.

11. If we turn our attention to those who spend their lives in the world, it becomes evident that the majority of them are inclined toward marriage. Indeed, they cannot be joined in matrimony if the parish priest, as is his duty, discovers through precise questioning that the man and the woman are ignorant of what is necessary for salvation.

    The bishop can scarcely permit such grave and ruinous ignorance to persist; he should remind the pastors of souls of their duty and, should they fail to fulfill it, address their negligence with appropriate disciplinary measures.

Teaching unto Penance

12. All people, regardless of age or social condition, are accustomed to cleansing the stains of the soul through the sacrament of penance. Therefore, the bishop must ensure that the priest who hears confessions holds as certain and immutable that sacramental absolution is invalid if imparted to someone who does not know what is necessary as a means of salvation. Moreover, men cannot be reconciled with God through this sacrament unless they are first brought, by dispelling the darkness of ignorance, to a knowledge of the Faith. The confessor must also know that absolution must be deferred in the case of one who, through their own fault, does not know what is necessary by precept. However, in such a case, the penitent may be absolved if they acknowledge their culpable but not insurmountable ignorance, ask God for forgiveness, and sincerely promise the confessor to strive, with God's help, to learn what is necessary by precept.

13. If, then, the pastors adopt this method of forming the Christian people, and direct their counsel, efforts, and intentions toward the

proposed approach, it is permissible to hope that the flock, through faith and good works, may advance over time to the point of being transformed into a dwelling of God in the Holy Spirit.

However, since this matter is of the utmost importance and no other institution has been established more conducive to the glory of God and the salvation of souls, no one should be surprised if countless obstacles are continually encountered.

Obstacles to Teaching

14. Sometimes, small and humble churches are located in the countryside, some near, others far from the parish church, where, on feast days, fathers of families with their children go to listen to the priest as he celebrates the Holy Mysteries. This results in their being rarely present in their parish and unable to hear any words concerning the mysteries of the Faith, the precepts, or the sacraments. The bishop must address this problem with the full weight of his authority. First, regarding the small churches near the parish, he must enact a precise law to prevent Mass from being celebrated there before the parish priest has himself celebrated, delivered the sermon, and fulfilled the remaining duties of his office. In this way, the parish church will be frequented by a multitude of faithful who will gather there. As for the small churches located far from the parish church, it is very difficult due to the distance for parishioners to avoid the nearest church and undertake a long and arduous journey, especially in winter when rivers overflow, to reach the parish and attend the Divine Offices, the bishop should decree, with the imposition of severe penalties, that the priests assigned to those churches instruct the people in the essential points of Christian doctrine and explain the divine law. However, the parish priest must be admonished not to place too much trust in the work of others, but to personally ensure the situation when it is required that the sacraments of the Eucharist and confirmation be administered to children, and when others request the sacrament of marriage.

15. Cities also present specific inconveniences. It often happens that in certain churches, especially those of religious orders, feasts are celebrated with solemn rites and large crowds. For this reason, if catechism is held in the parish church early in the morning or immediately after lunch, few or none will attend and will excuse themselves by citing the set time. If more convenient hours are not chosen for the people, experience confirms that the faithful will flock to the church where the feast day is solemnized, and, drawn by the liturgical display, will neglect Christian doctrine, to the grave detriment of their souls. Since it is not possible to establish a certain and general rule in this regard, we wish to leave this task to the diligent pastor of the church, who, taking into account the nature of the place, the circumstances, and the people, and weighing the overall significance of the situation, will find a way to harmonize the celebration of the feast day with Christian doctrine, so that one does not hinder the other. If the religious orders and exempted orders oppose this and, despite being admonished by the bishops, feel authorized to compromise the execution of Christian doctrine, we offer to the local ordinaries Our authority over the exempt orders, and the apostolic diligence will not lack other means to ensure that parish churches are not deprived of their due consideration.

16. It could prove highly beneficial for the education of the Christian people to appoint visitors, some of whom would travel around the city and others around the diocese, to conduct thorough investigations into all matters, allowing the bishop, once informed of the merits of each pastor, to decree rewards or punishments.

Adequate Texts and Methods

17. Following in the footsteps of Pope Clement VIII and Our other predecessors, we exhort in the Lord and strongly recommend that, in teaching Christian doctrine, the booklet written by Cardinal Bel-

larmine at the request of Pope Clement be used.[9] Carefully examined by the appropriate Congregation appointed for this purpose and approved, Pope Clement himself ordered that it be published, with the most valid intention that everyone thereafter adhere to the same and only method of teaching and learning Christian doctrine.

Nothing is more desirable than this uniformity, nothing more fitting and useful to prevent errors from stealthily creeping in amidst the diverse range of catechisms. If, in any place, it becomes necessary, due to specific local needs, to use another booklet, great care must be taken to ensure that it contains nothing contrary to Catholic truth. Attention must also be given to ensure that the dogmas of the Faith are explained in a simple and clear manner, with the addition of any necessary parts that may have been omitted, and the removal of the superfluous.

A concise and unified method of teaching is usually of great help for a simpler examination when assessing the progress of children.

18. This booklet must also contain the acts of faith, hope, and charity, certainly composed in a correct and competent manner. If this is not the case, once perfected, they should be printed in the proper form. These acts are better conveyed with concise rather than abundant words, provided that through them the full strength and nature of the virtue are revealed.

Since it is vitally necessary for those professing the Christian religion to have the habit and practice of frequently reciting these acts, so that their use is not confined to narrow limits or restricted by anyone to a modest number each year, the bishop, concerned with both his own and others' salvation, should issue appropriate provisions so that in the parishes of the city and diocese, pastors, immediately after the celebration of the feast day Mass, kneeling before the altar, clearly and intelligibly recite the aforementioned acts of the virtues,

[9] Editor's note: The so-called "short catechism" of St. Robert Bellarmine is included in Volume 2 of *Tradivox Catholic Catechism Index*, ed. Aaron Seng (Sophia Institute Press, 2020).

attempting to lead the people who must repeat the words they have spoken. In this way, the faithful, almost without realizing it, will learn them by heart and take up the habit of attending to this pious practice not only on feast days but also on the remaining days.

19. These salutary instructions for teaching the flock that we wished to make known to you, Venerable Brothers, through this apostolic letter of Ours, can be recognized by each of you as in conformity with Our pastoral warnings, already published with paternal love when we surrounded the Church of Bologna, our bride, with care.

These instructions are moreover derived from the Pontifical Constitutions, recognized as valid by the testimony and example of renowned bishops.

Since we know from experience that they will bring immense benefit, we exhort and encourage you with all possible fervor, and beseech you, by the bowels of the mercy of our God, to attend with steadfast and resolute hearts, in the strength of the task entrusted to your pastoral ministry, to the implementation of what has been proposed, carefully considering that all the labor, effort, and attention put forth for this purpose will be rewarded by God, the Giver of all good.

We cordially impart to you Our Apostolic Blessing.

Given in Rome at St. Mary Major, on the seventh of February 1742, in the second year of Our Pontificate.

Cum Religiosi

ENCYCLICAL ON CATECHESIS

Pope Benedict XIV

June 26, 1754

To the Patriarchs, Archbishops, and Bishops of Italy. Venerable Brothers, We give you Greeting and the Apostolic Blessing.

Removal of Impediments to Marriage

Religious men, devoted to the improvement of divine worship, have informed Us that it would be best to appoint special ministers in Our patriarchal basilicas, St. John Lateran, St. Peter's on the Vatican, and St. Mary Major's; their purpose would be to instruct those sent to these basilicas by the Apostolic Chancery to perform there the required servile works. These works are required before they are granted the object of their journey to Rome, which is the removal of an impediment to marriage. The aim of this instruction is to enable these people to be duly and beneficially cleansed by the sacrament of penance and to partake of the Sacrament of the Altar in a worthy manner. The Chancery demands that they receive both of these sacraments in addition to making the sacred pilgrimage to the seven churches and to ascending the holy stairway. We have issued timely orders on this subject before, as may be seen from Our encyclical letter of last January 16th to the cardinals who are archpriests of the said basilicas. We have subsequently been reliably informed of the great zeal shown in this important work by some of the canons and other clergy of the said basilicas; they constantly and eagerly press on with the careful carrying out of Our commands. Because of these reports, We have experienced a specially deep joy, and with all Our heart, have rendered due thanks to the most high God Who is the source of all good things.

Many Ignorant of the Mysteries of the Faith

1. We could not rejoice, however, when it was subsequently reported to Us that, in the course of religious instruction preparatory to confession and Holy Communion, it was very often found that these people were ignorant of the mysteries of the Faith, even of those matters which must be known by necessity of means; consequently, they were ineligible to partake of the sacraments.

Although the ministers mentioned continue unceasing instruction to eradicate this great evil, yet this evil greatly distresses the people requesting and waiting for their dispensation. For oppressed by poverty and begging for their food with their own hands, they wish to leave the city as quickly as possible, to return to their homelands and marry; this is the purpose of their journey, and they are undeterred by the discomforts of public and heavy penance.

Bishops Not at Fault

2. At the start of Our Pontificate, We wrote an encyclical letter[10] to increase the zeal of Our Venerable Brothers to ensure that in every diocese the elements and precepts of Christian doctrine be explained and learned. We have read both the old and new reports of their diocesan synods; We know they are filled with instructions and exhortations, and that they include everything helpful for transmitting Christian doctrine. Therefore, We heartily assert Our conviction that in this matter none of the bishops can be found lacking in the apostolic office entrusted to him; the fact that some members of their dioceses are ignorant is not due to their fault or negligence. It must clearly be attributed either to the obstinacy of their subjects who, despite the commands of their superiors, have avoided instruction in their Christian doctrine; they have, in fact, seldom

[10] *Ubi primum* (December 3, 1740).

if ever gathered to hear the Word of God explained in preaching. Or it could be attributed to the slowness of some for learning what is taught. Or perhaps it is because that although they learned the elements of Christian teaching in their earliest years, when they were older, they ceased learning and building upon the foundation of their youth. Because of this, they are gradually reduced to a state like that of people who were not taught in their early years or who never received instruction in Christian doctrine. Although these setbacks have continued in spite of every measure taken by Our Venerable Brothers, We must nonetheless stir up their zeal again by this encyclical letter. And they are obligated anew to take every step and care possible in this matter on which the eternal salvation of the souls entrusted to them depends.

Work of St. Charles Borromeo

3. Each one of you, Venerable Brothers, has thoroughly understood the measures taken by St. Charles Borromeo, both in his own large diocese of Milan and in the entire province of which he was metropolitan. He took these measures in order to establish a fruitful method of transmitting Christian doctrine, and he labored greatly in order to strongly sustain this religious education. And when he observed that his toil had not borne the fruit he desired, he did not despair, but instead increased his cares and concerns as is seen in the Fifth Synod of Milan: "We have hitherto shown great care in looking after the instruction of individual Christians in the fundamental doctrines in the Christian Faith; but since we realize that we have profited little so far, we are led by the importance of the matter to make these additional decisions." For it was enough for that holy prelate to see that the need still existed, and thus to address himself to the work a second time; in this endeavor, he added cares to cares and minimized the many measures he had employed up till then. In like manner, it was enough for the Assyrian king to be informed that the nations did not know the commands of God:

"And it was announced to the king of the Assyrians, and said: The nation which you transferred and sent to dwell in the cities of Samaria do not know the laws of God's land" (4 Kgs 17:26). He at once sent a priest to teach those nations the commands of God: "And the king of the Assyrians gave commands, saying: Bring there one of the priests which you led off as prisoners and let him go and dwell with them and teach them the laws of God's land" (4 Kgs 17:27).

Teach the Fundamentals of the Faith

4. Therefore with the example of St. Charles Borromeo before Us, We encourage you and implore you by the mercy of Jesus Christ not to despair in this important work of handing on the fundamentals of the Christian Faith, even if hitherto you have devoted all your zeal and care to it. See to it that every minister performs carefully the measures laid down by the holy Council of Trent and by the statutes of your synods: that on fixed days schoolmasters and mistresses should teach Christian doctrine; that confessors should perform this part of their duty whenever anyone stands at their tribunal who does not know what he must by necessity of means know to be saved; that priests should also provide this instruction before uniting spouses in marriage; that fathers of families and lords of houses should be gravely advised of the duty imposed on them of being themselves instructed and of seeing to the instruction in the commandments of Christian doctrine of their sons and of the members of their household; that the practice of reciting aloud properly composed acts of faith, hope, and charity by the priest and people before or after the parish Mass should be preserved in the dioceses in which it is customary and be carefully introduced where it is not. Parish priests should not avoid their duty of at least on feast days explaining the Gospel to the people from the altar when there is no sermon. In addition, they are obliged to teach them the chief mysteries of our holy religion, the commandments of God and the Church, and everything which is necessary for their worthy par-

taking of the sacraments. Preachers should also follow this path, recalling the salutary advice that they should join instruction to exhortation whenever their hearers stand in need of both. Finally, the best method for instructing ignorant men in Christian doctrine is indicated by St. Augustine, who says that the most fruitful procedure is to ask questions in a friendly fashion after the explanation; from this questioning one can learn whether each one understood what he heard or whether the explanation needs repeating. In order that the learner grasp the matter, "we must ascertain by questioning whether the one being catechized has understood, and in accordance with his response, we must either explain more clearly and fully or not dwell further on what is known to them, etc. But if a man is very slow, he must be mercifully helped and the most necessary doctrines especially should be briefly imparted to him."[11]

We are assured that you yourselves will pursue many more paths than We point out to you in this encyclical letter. In the meantime, Venerable Brothers, We lovingly impart to you and to the flock entrusted to your care Our Apostolic Blessing.

Given at Castel Gandolfo on the twenty-sixth of June 1754, in the fourteenth year of Our Pontificate.

[11] St. Augustine, *De catechizandis rudibus*, chap. 13.

In Dominico Agro

ENCYCLICAL ON INSTRUCTION IN THE FAITH

Pope Clement XIII

June 14, 1761

To the Venerable Brothers, the Patriarchs, Primates, Archbishops, and Bishops. Venerable Brothers, Greetings and Apostolic Benediction.

1. In the Lord's field, for the tending of which divine Providence placed Us as overseer, there is nothing which demands as much vigilant care and unremitting labor in its cultivation than guarding the good seed of Catholic teaching which the apostles received from Jesus Christ and handed on to Us. If in laziness this is neglected, the enemy of the human race will sow weeds while the workers sleep. Then weeds will be found which should be committed to the flames rather than good grain to store in the barns.

However, St. Paul strongly encourages Us to protect the Faith that the saints handed on to Us (see Heb 3). He told Timothy to preserve the sacred trust (see 2 Tm 1:14) because dangerous times were coming (see 2 Tm 3:1) when evil and deceitful men would exist in the Church of God (2 Tm 3:13). The insidious tempters would use their work to try to infect unwary minds with errors which are hostile to evangelical truth.

Difficulty of Making Doctrinal Statements

2. It often happens that certain unworthy ideas come forth in the Church of God which, although they directly contradict each other, plot together to undermine the purity of the Catholic Faith in some way. It is very difficult to cautiously balance our speech be-

tween both enemies in such a way that We seem to turn Our backs on none of them, but to shun and condemn both enemies of Christ equally. Meanwhile the matter is such that diabolical error, when it has artfully colored its lies, easily clothes itself in the likeness of truth while very brief additions or changes corrupt the meaning of expressions; and confession, which usually works salvation, sometimes, with a slight change, inches toward death.

Limits of Instruction

3. The faithful—especially those who are simple or uncultivated—should be kept away from dangerous and narrow paths upon which they can hardly set foot without faltering. The sheep should not be led to pasture through trackless places. Nor should peculiar ideas—even those of Catholic scholars—be proposed to them. Rather, only those ideas should be communicated which are definitely marked as Catholic truth by their universality, ambiguity, and harmony. Besides, since the crowd cannot go up to the mountain (see Ex 19:12) upon which the glory of the Lord came down, and if whoever crosses the boundaries to see will die, the teachers of the people should establish boundaries around them so that no word strays beyond that which is necessary or useful for salvation. The faithful should obey the apostolic advice not to know more than is necessary, but to know in moderation (see Rom 12:3).

4. The popes clearly understood this. They devoted all their efforts not only to cut short with the sword of anathema the poisonous buds of growing error, but also to cut away certain developing ideas which either could prevent the Christian people unnecessarily from bearing a greater fruit of faith or could harm the minds of the faithful by their proximity to error. So the Council of Trent condemned those heresies which tried at that time to dim the light of the Church and which led Catholic truth into a clearer light as if the cloud of errors had been dispersed. As Our predecessors

understood that that holy meeting of the universal Church was so prudent in judgment and so moderate that it abstained from condemning ideas which authorities among Church scholars supported, they wanted another work prepared with the agreement of that holy council which would cover the entire teaching which the faithful should know and which would be far removed from any error. They printed and distributed this book under the title of the Roman Catechism.[12]

Excellence of the Roman Catechism

There are aspects of their action worthy of special praise. In it they compiled the teaching which is common to the whole Church and which is far removed from every danger of error, and they proposed to transmit it openly to the faithful in very eloquent words according to the precept of Christ the Lord who told the apostles to proclaim in the light what He had said in the dark and to proclaim from the rooftops what they heard in secret (see Mt 10:27). They have obeyed His Bride, the Church, whose words are: "Show me ... where You recline at midday" (Cant 1:7). For where it is not midday and the light is not so bright that truth can be clearly known, error can easily be mistaken for truth because of its appearance of truth, and can be distinguished from truth only with difficulty in the darkness. They knew that there were before and would again be people who attract those who seek food by the promise of more abundant pastures of wisdom and knowledge and that many people would come to those pastures because "stolen waters are sweeter and hidden bread more delightful" (Prv 9:17).

Therefore, in case the Church should be deceived and wander after the flocks of the companions who are themselves wanderers and unsettled with no certainty of truth, who are always learning but never arriving at the knowledge of truth (see 2 Tm 3:7), they

[12] Editor's note: The Catechism of the Council of Trent, often referred to simply as "the Roman Catechism," is included in Volume 7 of *Tradivox Catholic Catechism Index*, ed. Aaron Seng (Sophia Institute Press, 2021).

proposed that only what is necessary and very useful for salvation be clearly and plainly explained in the Roman Catechism and communicated to the faithful.

5. But even though this book, composed with remarkable work and effort, was universally approved and welcomed with the highest praises, at that time, the love of novelty almost wrested it from the priests' hands by inspiring the production of more and more catechisms which could compare in no way with the Roman Catechism. Thus two evils arose. Agreement on a method of teaching was almost destroyed, and the weak members of the faithful were scandalized at finding that they were no longer united by the same language and topics (see Gn 11). On the other hand, contentions arose from different ways of transmitting Catholic truth and disunity of spirit and great disagreements from rivalry, while one declared he was a follower of Apollo, another of Cephas, and another of Paul. We think that nothing can be more fatal to God's greater glory than the bitterness of those disagreements. Nothing can eliminate more disastrously the fruits which the faithful should gain from Christian discipline.

Reissue of the Roman Catechism

Thus, in order to remove the double evil from the Church, We must return to that method from which some, setting themselves up in the Church as wiser, have insolently and imprudently led the faithful away for some time. We think that the Roman Catechism should be offered to the priests again so that just as it once strengthened the Catholic Faith and strengthened the minds of the faithful in the Church's teaching which is the "pillar of truth" (1 Tm 3:15), it may now turn them away from new ideas which neither antiquity nor unanimity recommend. To make the book more easily accessible and to correct the errors which have occurred in course of production, We have ensured that the copy published by Our predecessor St. Pius V in accordance with the decree of the Council of Trent is reprinted in Rome with all care. The vernacular translation of it which was made and published by order of the same St. Pius will be reprinted very soon by Our order and will finally be published.

6. So since Our care and diligence are providing a very suitable aid to remove the deceptions of wicked ideas at this very difficult time for the Church and to spread and establish true and sound teaching, it is your duty to see to it that the faithful accept it. Because the popes wanted this book set before pastors almost as the norm of Catholic faith and Christian discipline in order that unanimity might exist also in the method of transmitting doctrine, We now strongly recommend it to you, Venerable Brothers. We strongly encourage you to order that everybody who has the care of souls should use it in instructing the faithful in the Catholic truth in order to preserve unity of learning, charity, and harmony of spirits. For it is your duty to be attentive to everybody's serenity. Finally, it is the bishop's duty to watch carefully that nobody breaks the bond of unity and creates schisms by proudly acting in his own interests.

Qualities of the Good Teacher

7. If those who ought to present and explain these books to the faithful are unsuitable teachers, they will prove useless or almost useless. Therefore, it is of the utmost importance that you choose for the office of communicating Christian teaching to the faithful not only men endowed with theological knowledge, but more importantly, men who manifest humility, enthusiasm for sanctifying souls, and charity. The totality of Christian practice does not consist in abundance of words, nor in skill of debating, nor in the search from praise and glory, but in true and voluntary humility. There are those whom a greater wisdom raises up but also separates from the society of other people. The more they know, the more they dislike the virtue of harmony. Wisdom itself warns them with the Word of God: "Have salt in yourselves and be at peace among us" (Mk

9:49). Thus it is necessary to have the salt of wisdom to preserve the love of neighbor and to offset weaknesses. If they turn from zeal for wisdom and from concern for their neighbor to disagreement, they have salt without peace—not a gift of virtue but a cause for condemnation. The more they know, the worse they fail. The apostle James condemns them with these words: "If you are jealous and have contentions in your hearts, do not boast and be liars against the truth. This wisdom did not come down from on high. Rather, it is earthly, animal, diabolical. Inconstancy and every wicked deed accompany jealousy and contention. The wisdom which comes from on high is first of all pure. Then it is peaceful, modest, persuasive, agreeable to good things, full of mercy and good fruits. It does not judge and is without rivalry" (Jas 3:14–17).

8. Therefore, while We pray to God in affliction of spirit and in humility of heart to bestow His indulgence and mercy on our efforts to prevent disagreement disturbing the faithful, and to ensure that, in the bond of peace and in charity of spirit, we all know, praise, and glorify the one God and Our Lord Jesus Christ, We greet you with a holy kiss and We lovingly impart Our Apostolic Blessing to all of you and to all the faithful of your churches.

Given at Castel Gandolfo on the fourteenth day of June 1761, the third year of Our Pontificate.

Probe Nostis

APOSTOLIC BRIEF ON THE PROPAGATION OF THE FAITH

Pope Gregory XVI

September 18, 1840

To the Patriarchs, Archbishops, and Bishops of Italy. Venerable Brothers, We give you Greeting and Our Apostolic Blessing.

1. You are well aware, Venerable Brothers, of the many misfortunes which now afflict the Catholic Church. You know, too, that holy religion is being attacked by the pollution of errors of every kind and by the unbridled rashness of renegades. At the same time, heretics and unbelievers attempt by cleverness and deceit to pervert the hearts and minds of the faithful. You are aware, in short, that practically no effort has been left untried in the attempt to overthrow the unshakeable building of the holy city. In particular, We are obliged, alas! to see the wicked enemies of truth spread everywhere unpunished. They harass religion with ridicule, the Church with insults, and Catholics with arrogance and calumny. They even enter cities and towns, establish schools of error and impiety, and publish their poisonous teachings which are adapted to secret deceit by misusing the natural sciences and recent discoveries. Furthermore, they enter the hovels of the poor, traverse the countryside, and seek the acquaintance of the farmers and the lowest classes. They try every method of attracting the uneducated, especially the youth, to their sects, and of making them desert the Catholic Faith, whether by means of Bibles inaccurately translated into the vernacular, pestilential newspapers and pamphlets of lit-

tle weight, or by seductive speeches, pretended charity, and gifts of money.

ACTIVITIES OF HERETICS

2. We mention events which you yourselves witness. For despite your sorrow and your pastoral denunciations, you are obliged to tolerate in your dioceses these men spreading heresy and unbelief, these assertive preachers who ceaselessly waylay and ravage your flock by going around in sheep's clothing while inwardly they are ravening wolves. What more can We add? There is hardly any uncivilized district left in the entire world to which headquarters of the main societies of heretics and unbelievers have not sent scouts and emissaries without counting the cost. These men, by waging secret or open war on the Catholic religion and its pastors and ministers, tear the faithful from the bosom of the Church and prevent unbelievers from entering it.

3. You can easily imagine the straits in which We live, since We are laden with the care of Christ's flock and the churches, and must therefore render a detailed account to the divine Prince of Shepherds. For this reason, We decided to recall in this letter the causes of the troubles which beset both Us and you. You can then reflect how important it is for all the bishops to redouble their efforts so as to break the assault of the enemies, to beat back their attacks, and to forewarn and protect the faithful from their clever appeals. We have been doing this, and We shall not stop. We know that you have likewise done so, and We are confident that you will continue.

CHRIST'S PROMISES OF HELP

4. However, in order not to lose heart:

> We should all be sure not to fear them as if We had to overcome them by our own strength, since Christ is both our counsel and our courage. As we can do nothing without Him, with Him we can

do all things. To give strength to the preachers of the Gospel and ministers of the sacraments, He says, "Behold I am with you all days even to the end of the world" (Mt 28:20), and also, "I have spoken these things to you that you may have peace in Me; in the world you shall have affliction but take heart, I have overcome the world" (Jn 16:33). So clear and indisputable are these promises that no scandals should make us weak lest we seem unthankful for God's choice of us even though His help is as effective as His promises are true.[13]

5. Even in our time all can see those clear results of the divine promise which never have failed and never shall fail in the Church. They are plainly seen in the unconquerable constancy of the Church amid so many enemy attacks, in the spread of religion amid such disturbance and dangers, and in the consolation which "the Father of mercies and the God of all consolation gives us in every trial" (2 Cor 1:3–4). On the one hand, We have to lament the loss which the Catholic religion has suffered and continues to suffer in certain districts. But the many victories which the unconquerable constancy of Catholics and their priests has won and continues to win even in those districts gives us ground for joy. We rejoice greatly also at its marvelously abundant gains despite so many hindrances. This proves even to our enemies that oppression of the Church frequently contributes to its glory and strengthens the faithful.

Apostolic Missions

6. We are thankful for the success of apostolic missions in America, the Indies, and other faithless lands. The indefatigable zeal of many apostolic men has led them abroad into those places. Relying not on wealth nor on any army, they are protected by the shield of faith alone. They fearlessly "fight the Lord's battles" (cf. 1 Kgs 25:28) against heresy and unbelief by private and public speech and writings. They are inspired with a burning love and undeterred by

[13] Pope St. Leo the Great, *Ep.* 167, *ad Rusticum*, chap. 2.

rough roads and heavy toil. They search out those who sit in darkness and the shadow of death to summon them to the light and life of the Catholic religion. So fearless in the face of every danger, they bravely enter the woods and caves of savages, gradually pacify them by Christian kindness, and prepare them for true faith and real virtue. At length they snatch them from the devil's rule by the bath of regeneration, and promote them to the freedom of God's adopted sons.

Martyrs in the Far East

7. However, We are reduced to tears both of sorrow in Our detestation of cruel persecutors and executioners, and of consolation in beholding the heroic constancy of the confessors of the Faith, as We recall here the glorious deeds of the new martyrs in the Far East. We have already praised them at length in an address to the consistory.[14] Tonkin and Cochin are still wet with the blood of many bishops, priests, and faithful. They have repeated the achievement of the early Christian martyrs in facing a cruel death for Christ undismayed by torture. This is a major victory for the Church and for religion. It casts the persecutors into confusion when they see that even today the divine promises of unending protection and help are really fulfilled. This is the reason why, in the words of St. Leo: "The religion established by the sacrament of the Cross of Christ cannot be destroyed by any kind of cruelty."[15]

New Societies Working for Catholicism

8. These events bring consolation and glory to the Catholic religion. But there are other grounds of consolation for the Church. Pious organizations are developing for the good of religion and Christian society. Some of these assist the work of the holy apostolic missions. God, who ceaselessly protects His Church, raises up within

[14] Allocution *Afflictas in Tunquino* (April 27, 1840).

[15] *Serm.* 82 (80), *In natali apostolorum Petri et Pauli*, chap. 6.

it new societies as times, places, and circumstances require. Under the Church's authority, each society in its own ways devotes its full energy to works of charity, the instruction of the faithful, and the spread of the Faith.

9. Likewise a source of joy to the Catholic world, and a wonder to non-Catholics, are the many widespread sodalities of pious women. Under the rule of St. Vincent de Paul or in association with other approved institutes, they are remarkable in their practice of the Christian virtues. They devote themselves entirely either to saving women from the way of perdition, or to training girls in religion, solid piety, and the tasks suited to their state in life, or to relieving the dire want of their neighbors with every assistance. No natural weakness of their sex or fear of any danger holds them back.

10. A similar cause of joy for Us and for all good men are those groups of the faithful who recently have begun to meet regularly in many cities, especially the larger ones. Their purpose is to combat bad books with good ones written by themselves or others, displaying purity of doctrine instead of foul forms of error, and Christian gentleness and charity instead of insults and attacks.

Society for the Propagation of the Faith

11. Finally We must praise most highly the well-known society which is constantly expanding, not alone in Catholic territories but even in the countries of non-Catholics and unbelievers. This society enables the faithful of every class to help the apostolic missions and to have a share themselves in the spiritual graces of these missions. We are referring, as you realize, to the famous Society for the Propagation of the Faith.

12. Now you know both the sorrows which afflict Us for Our losses and of the consolations which sustain Us in the victories of the

Catholic religion. We are concerned though that these societies should continue to grow. We earnestly urge you, then, to cherish, protect, and augment them in your own dioceses.

13. The principal society which We recommend to you is the Society for the Propagation of the Faith. First organized in Lyons in 1822, it spread with marvelous speed and success. But, certainly, We recommend equally other societies of this type founded at Vienna and elsewhere. Their names are different, but they work at the same task of the propagation of the Faith, a task which enjoys the religious support and favor of Catholic princes. This task is sustained and strengthened by the moderate offerings and daily prayers to God said by each of the members. It is directed to supporting the apostolic workers, to practicing the works of Christian charity toward neophytes, and to delivering the faithful from the attack of persecution. Consequently, We consider it deserving of the admiration and love of all good men. A work so beneficial to the Church can have begun so recently only by the special design of divine Providence. For when every kind of plot of the infernal enemy besets the beloved Spouse of Christ, the Church could have no more timely good fortune than this ardent desire of the faithful to spread Catholic truth.

14. For this reason, established as We are despite Our unworthiness in the Papacy, We Ourselves affirm with Our predecessors Our complete support for this great work. Sharing Our concern, you should see to it that this important work flourishes among your flock. "Sing with the trumpet in Sion" (Jl 2:1) and by your fatherly advice see to it that those not already members of the pious society are eager to become members, and that those who are members persevere in their purpose.

15. This is surely the time "when the Christian battle line should smash the devil as he rages all over the world";[16] it is indeed the time for the faithful to join in this holy union with the priests. We have the strongest hope that God, Who ceaselessly supports His Church in its long hard fight with its enemies and also gives it joy in the firmness, love, and devotion of the faithful, will grant it the peace it desires when He is placated by Our combined prayers and pious works.

In the meantime We lovingly impart the Apostolic Blessing to yourselves, Venerable Brothers, and to all the clergy and lay faithful entrusted to your charge.

Given in Rome at St. Mary Major with the seal of the fisherman on the eighteenth day of September 1840, in the tenth year of Our Pontificate.

[16] Pope St. Leo the Great, *Serm.* 49, *De Quadragesima*, chap. 3.

Quanta Cura

ENCYCLICAL CONDEMNING CURRENT ERRORS

Pope Pius IX

December 8, 1864

To Our Venerable Brethren, all Patriarchs, Primates, Archbishops, and Bishops having favor and communion of the Holy See. Venerable Brethren, Health and Apostolic Benediction.

Apostolic Duty to Condemn Heresy

1. With how great care and pastoral vigilance the Roman Pontiffs, Our predecessors, fulfilling the duty and office committed to them by the Lord Christ Himself in the person of most blessed Peter, Prince of the Apostles, of feeding the lambs and the sheep, have never ceased sedulously to nourish the Lord's whole flock with words of faith and with salutary doctrine, and to guard it from poisoned pastures, is thoroughly known to all, and especially to you, Venerable Brethren. And truly the same, Our predecessors, asserters as they were and vindicators of the august Catholic religion, of truth, and of justice, being specially anxious for the salvation of souls, had nothing ever more at heart than by their most wise letters and constitutions to unveil and condemn all those heresies and errors which, being adverse to our divine Faith, to the doctrine of the Catholic Church, to purity of morals, and to the eternal salvation of men, have frequently excited violent tempests, and have miserably afflicted both Church and State. For which cause the same Our predecessors have, with apostolic fortitude, constantly resisted the nefarious enterprises of wicked men, who, like raging waves of the sea foaming out their own confusion, and promising liberty whereas they are the slaves of corruption, have striven

by their deceptive opinions and most pernicious writings to raze the foundations of the Catholic religion and of civil society, to remove from among men all virtue and justice, to deprave the mind and judgment of all, to turn away from true moral training unwary persons, and especially inexperienced youth, miserably to corrupt such youth, to lead it into the snares of error, and at length tear it from the bosom of the Catholic Church.

2. But now, as is well known to you, Venerable Brethren, already, scarcely had we been elevated to this Chair of Peter (by the hidden counsel of divine Providence, certainly by no merits of Our own), when, seeing with the greatest grief of Our soul a truly awful storm excited by so many evil opinions, and [seeing also] the most grievous calamities never sufficiently to be deplored which overspread the Christian people from so many errors, according to the duty of Our Apostolic Ministry, and following the illustrious example of Our predecessors, We raised Our voice, and in many published encyclical letters and allocutions delivered in consistory, and other apostolic letters, we condemned the chief errors of this our most unhappy age, and we excited your admirable episcopal vigilance, and we again and again admonished and exhorted all sons of the Catholic Church, to Us most dear, that they should altogether abhor and flee from the contagion of so dire a pestilence. And especially in Our first encyclical letter written to you on November 9, 1846,[17] and in two allocutions delivered by Us in consistory, the one on December 9, 1854,[18] and the other on June 9, 1862,[19] we condemned the monstrous portents of opinion which prevail especially in this age, bringing with them the greatest loss of souls and detriment of civil society itself; which are grievously opposed also, not only to the Catholic Church and her salutary doctrine and venerable rights, but also to the eternal natural law engraven

17 *Qui pluribus.*

18 *Singulari quadam.*

19 *Maxima quidem.*

by God in all men's hearts, and to right reason; and from which almost all other errors have their origin.

ERRORS OF NATURALISM

3. But, although we have not omitted often to proscribe and reprobate the chief errors of this kind, yet the cause of the Catholic Church, and the salvation of souls entrusted to us by God, and the welfare of human society itself, altogether demand that we again stir up your pastoral solicitude to exterminate other evil opinions, which spring forth from the said errors as from a fountain. Which false and perverse opinions are on that ground the more to be detested, because they chiefly tend to this, that that salutary influence be impeded and [even] removed which the Catholic Church, according to the institution and command of her divine Author, should freely exercise even to the end of the world—not only over private individuals, but over nations, peoples, and their sovereign princes; and [tend also] to take away that mutual fellowship and concord of counsels between Church and State which has ever proved itself propitious and salutary, both for religious and civil interests.[20] For you well know, Venerable Brethren, that at this time men are found not a few who, applying to civil society the impious and absurd principle of naturalism, as they call it, dare to teach that "the best constitution of public society and [also] civil progress altogether require that human society be conducted and governed without regard being had to religion any more than if it did not exist; or, at least, without any distinction being made between the true religion and false ones." And, against the doctrine of Scripture, of the Church, and of the holy Fathers, they do not hesitate to assert that "that is the best condition of society, in which no duty is recognized, as attached to the civil power, of restraining, by enacted penalties, offenders against the Catholic religion, except so far as public peace may require." From which totally false idea of social

20 See Pope Gregory XVI, Encyclical *Mirari vos* (August 15, 1832).

government they do not fear to foster that erroneous opinion, most fatal in its effects on the Catholic Church and the salvation of souls, called by Our predecessor, Gregory XVI, an "insanity," viz., that "liberty of conscience and worship is each man's personal right, which ought to be legally proclaimed and asserted in every rightly constituted society; and that a right resides in the citizens to an absolute liberty, which should be restrained by no authority, whether ecclesiastical or civil, whereby they may be able openly and publicly to manifest and declare any of their ideas whatever, either by word of mouth, by the press, or in any other way."[21] But, while they rashly affirm this, they do not think and consider that they are preaching the "liberty of perdition";[22] and that "if human arguments are always allowed free room for discussion, there will never be wanting men who will dare to resist truth, and to trust in the flowing speech of human wisdom; whereas we know, from the very teaching of Our Lord Jesus Christ, how carefully Christian faith and wisdom should avoid this most injurious babbling."[23]

Liberalism, Communism, and Socialism

4. And, since where religion has been removed from civil society, and the doctrine and authority of divine revelation repudiated, the genuine notion itself of justice and human right is darkened and lost, and the place of true justice and legitimate right is supplied by material force, thence it appears why it is that some, utterly neglecting and disregarding the surest principles of sound reason, dare to proclaim that "the people's will, manifested by what is called public opinion or in some other way, constitutes a supreme law, free from all divine and human control, and that in the political order accomplished facts, from the very circumstance that they are accomplished, have the force of right." But who does not see and

[21] Pope Gregory XVI, *Mirari vos*, no. 14.

[22] St. Augustine, *Ep.* 105 (166), chap. 2.

[23] Pope St. Leo the Great, *Ep.* 14 (133), sect. 2, edit. Ball.

clearly perceive that human society, when set loose from the bonds of religion and true justice, can have, in truth, no other end than the purpose of obtaining and amassing wealth, and that [society under such circumstances] follows no other law in its actions, except the unchastened desire of ministering to its own pleasures and interests? For this reason, men of the kind pursue with bitter hatred the religious orders, although these have deserved extremely well of Christendom, civilization, and literature, and cry out that the same have no legitimate reason for being permitted to exist; and thus [these evil men] applaud the calumnies of heretics. For, as Pius VI, Our predecessor, taught most wisely: "The abolition of regulars is injurious to that state in which the evangelical counsels are openly professed; it is injurious to a method of life praised in the Church as agreeable to apostolic doctrine; it is injurious to the illustrious founders themselves, whom we venerate on our altars, who did not establish these societies but by God's inspiration."[24] And [these wretches] also impiously declare that permission should be refused to citizens and to the Church, "whereby they may openly give alms for the sake of Christian charity"; and that the law should be abrogated "whereby on certain fixed days servile works are prohibited because of God's worship"; on the most deceptive pretext that the said permission and law are opposed to the principles of the best public economy. Moreover, not content with removing religion from public society, they wish to banish it also from private families. For teaching and professing the most fatal error of Communism and Socialism, they assert that "domestic society or the family derives the whole principle of its existence from the civil law alone; and consequently that from the civil law alone issue, and on it depend, all rights of parents over their children, and especially that of providing for education." By which impious opinions and machinations these most deceitful men chiefly aim at this result, viz., that the salutary teaching and influence of the Catholic Church may be

[24] Brief *Quod aliquantum* (March 10, 1791).

entirely banished from the instruction and education of youth, and that the tender and flexible minds of young men may be infected and depraved by every most pernicious error and vice. For all who have endeavored to throw into confusion things both sacred and secular, and to subvert the right order of society, and to abolish all rights divine and human, have always (as we above hinted) devoted all their nefarious schemes, devices, and efforts, to deceiving and depraving incautious youth, and have placed all their hope in its corruption. For which reason they never cease by every wicked method to assail the clergy, both secular and regular, from whom (as the surest monuments of history conspicuously attest), so many great advantages have abundantly flowed to Christianity, civilization, and literature, and to proclaim that "the clergy, as being hostile to the true and beneficial advance of science and civilization, should be removed from the whole charge and duty of instructing and educating youth."

Denial of the Authority of the Church

5. Others meanwhile, reviving the wicked and so often condemned inventions of innovators, dare with signal impudence to subject to the will of the civil authority the supreme authority of the Church and of this Apostolic See given to her by Christ Himself, and to deny all those rights of the same Church and See which concern matters of the external order. For they are not ashamed of affirming "that the Church's laws do not bind in conscience unless when they are promulgated by the civil power; that acts and decrees of the Roman Pontiffs, referring to religion and the Church, need the civil power's sanction and approbation, or at least its consent; that the apostolic constitutions,[25] whereby secret societies are condemned (whether an oath of secrecy be or be not required in such

[25] See Pope Clement XII, Bull *In eminenti* (April 28, 1738); Pope Benedict XIV, Bull *Providas Romanorum* (March 18, 1751); Pope Pius VII, Bull *Ecclesiam a Jesu* (September 13, 1821); and Pope Leo XII, Bull *Quo graviora* (March 13, 1825).

societies), and whereby their frequenters and favorites are smitten with anathema, have no force in those regions of the world wherein associations of the kind are tolerated by the civil government; that the excommunication pronounced by the Council of Trent and by Roman Pontiffs against those who assail and usurp the Church's rights and possessions rests on a confusion between the spiritual and temporal orders, and [is directed] to the pursuit of a purely secular good; that the Church can decree nothing which binds the consciences of the faithful in regard to their use of temporal things; that the Church has no right of restraining by temporal punishments those who violate her laws; that it is conformable to the principles of sacred theology and public law to assert and claim for the civil government a right of property in those goods which are possessed by the Church, by the religious orders, and by other pious establishments." Nor do they blush openly and publicly to profess the maxim and principle of heretics from which arise so many perverse opinions and errors. For they repeat that "the ecclesiastical power is not by divine right distinct from, and independent of, the civil power, and that such distinction and independence cannot be preserved without the civil power's essential rights being assailed and usurped by the Church." Nor can we pass over in silence the audacity of those who, not enduring sound doctrine, contend that, "without sin and without any sacrifice of the Catholic profession, assent and obedience may be refused to those judgments and decrees of the Apostolic See, whose object is declared to concern the Church's general good, and her rights and discipline, so only it do not touch the dogmata of faith and morals." But no one can be found not clearly and distinctly to see and understand how grievously this is opposed to the Catholic dogma of the full power given from God by Christ Our Lord Himself to the Roman Pontiff of feeding, ruling, and guiding the universal Church.

Condemnation of Errors

6. Amidst, therefore, such great perversity of depraved opinions, We, well remembering Our Apostolic Office, and very greatly solicitous for our most holy religion, for sound doctrine and the salvation of souls which is entrusted to Us by God, and [solicitous also] for the welfare of human society itself, have thought it right again to raise up Our Apostolic voice. Therefore, by Our Apostolic authority we reprobate, proscribe, and condemn all and singular the evil opinions and doctrines severally mentioned in this letter, and will and command that they be thoroughly held by all children of the Catholic Church as reprobated, proscribed, and condemned.

7. And besides these things, you know very well, Venerable Brethren, that in these times the haters of all truth and justice and most bitter enemies of our religion, deceiving the people and maliciously lying, disseminate sundry other impious doctrines by means of pestilential books, pamphlets, and newspapers dispersed over the whole world. Nor are you ignorant, also, that in this our age some men are found who, moved and excited by the spirit of Satan, have reached to that degree of impiety as not to shrink from denying Our Ruler and Lord Jesus Christ, and from impugning His divinity with wicked pertinacity. Here, however, we cannot but extol you, Venerable Brethren, with great and deserved praise, for not having failed to raise, with all zeal, your episcopal voice against impiety so great.

Pastoral Duty to Teach

8. Therefore, in this Our letter, we again most lovingly address you, who, having been called unto a part of Our solicitude, are to Us, among our grievous distresses, the greatest solace, joy, and consolation, because of the admirable religion and piety wherein you excel, and because of that marvelous love, fidelity, and dutifulness, whereby, bound as you are to Us, and to this Apostolic See in most

harmonious affection, you strive strenuously and sedulously to fulfill your most weighty episcopal ministry. For from your signal pastoral zeal we expect that, taking up the sword of the spirit which is the word of God, and strengthened in the grace of Our Lord Jesus Christ, you will, with redoubled care, each day more anxiously provide that the faithful entrusted to your charge "abstain from noxious herbage, which Jesus Christ does not cultivate because it is not His Father's plantation."[26] Never cease also to inculcate on the said faithful that all true felicity flows abundantly upon man from our august religion and its doctrine and practice; and that "happy is the people whose God is their Lord" (Ps 143:15). Teach that "kingdoms rest on the foundation of the Catholic Faith,[27] and that nothing is so deadly, so hastening to a fall, so exposed to all danger [as that which exists] if, believing this alone to be sufficient for us that we received free will at our birth, we seek nothing further from the Lord; that is, if forgetting our Creator we abjure His power that we may display our freedom."[28] And again do not fail to teach that "the royal power was given not only for the governance of the world, but most of all for the protection of the Church";[29] and that there is nothing which can be of greater advantage and glory to princes and kings than if, as another most wise and courageous predecessor of Ours, St. Felix, instructed the Emperor Zeno, they "permit the Catholic Church to practice her laws, and allow no one to oppose her liberty. For it is certain that this mode of conduct is beneficial to their interests, viz., that where there is question concerning the causes of God, they study, according to His appointment, to subject the royal will to Christ's priests, not to raise it above theirs."[30]

26 St. Ignatius of Antioch, *Ep. ad Philadelph.*, chap. 3.

27 See Pope St. Celestine, *Ep.* 22 to the Council of Ephesus (431).

28 Pope St. Innocent I, *Ep.* 29 to the bishops of the Council of Carthage (416).

29 Pope St. Leo the Great, *Ep.* 156 (125), chap. 3.

30 See Pope Pius VII, Encyclical *Diu satis*, (May 15, 1800), no. 18.

Necessity of Prayer

9. But if always, Venerable Brethren, now most of all amidst such great calamities both of the Church and of civil society, amidst so great a conspiracy against Catholic interests and this Apostolic See, and so great a mass of errors, it is altogether necessary to approach with confidence the throne of grace, that We may obtain mercy and find grace in timely aid. Wherefore, We have thought it well to excite the piety of all the faithful in order that, together with Us and you, they may unceasingly pray and beseech the most merciful Father of light and pity with most fervent and humble prayers, and in the fullness of faith flee always to Our Lord Jesus Christ, Who redeemed us to God in His blood, and earnestly and constantly supplicate His most sweet Heart, the Victim of most burning love toward us, that He would draw all things to Himself by the bonds of His love, and that all men inflamed by His most holy love may walk worthily according to His Heart, pleasing God in all things, bearing fruit in every good work. But since without doubt men's prayers are more pleasing to God if they reach Him from minds free of all stain, therefore we have determined to open to Christ's faithful, with apostolic liberality, the Church's heavenly treasures committed to our charge, in order that the said faithful, being more earnestly enkindled to true piety, and cleansed through the sacrament of penance from the defilement of their sins, may with greater confidence pour forth their prayers to God, and obtain His mercy and grace.

10. By these letters therefore, in virtue of Our Apostolic authority, We concede to all and singular the faithful of the Catholic world, a plenary indulgence in form of Jubilee, during the space of one month only for the whole coming year 1865, and not beyond; to be fixed by you, Venerable Brethren, and other legitimate ordinaries of places, in the very same manner and form in which We granted it at the beginning of Our Supreme Pontificate by Our apostolic let-

ters in the form of a Brief, dated November 20, 1846, and addressed to all your episcopal order, beginning, "Arcano Divinae Providentiae consilio," and with all the same faculties which were given by Us in those letters. We will, however, that all things be observed which were prescribed in the aforesaid letters, and those things be excepted which We there so declared. And We grant this, notwithstanding anything whatever to the contrary, even things which are worthy of individual mention and derogation. In order however that all doubt and difficulty be removed, We have commanded a copy of the said letters to be sent you.

Blessed Virgin Mary, Destroyer of All Heresies

11. "Let us implore," Venerable Brethren, "God's mercy from our inmost heart and with our whole mind: because He has Himself added, 'I will not remove My mercy from them' (cf. Ps 88:34). Let us ask and we shall receive; and if there be delay and slowness in our receiving because we have gravely offended, let us knock, because 'to him that knocketh it shall be opened' (Lk 11:10), if only the door be knocked by our prayers, groans, and tears, in which we must persist and persevere, and if the prayer be unanimous:... let each man pray to God, not for himself alone, but for all his brethren, as the Lord hath taught us to pray."[31] But in order that God may the more readily assent to the prayers and desires of Ourselves, of you, and of all the faithful, let us with all confidence employ as our advocate with Him the immaculate and most holy Virgin Mary, Mother of God, who has slain all heresies throughout the world, and who, the most loving Mother of us all, "is all sweet ... and full of mercy ... shows herself to all as easily entreated: shows herself to all as most merciful; pities the necessities of all with a most large affection";[32] and standing as a Queen at the right hand of her only begotten Son, Our Lord Jesus Christ, in gilded clothing, surrounded

[31] St. Cyprian, *Ep.* 7, chaps. 2, 7.

[32] St. Bernard, *Serm. de duodecim praerogativis B. M. V. ex verbis Apocalyp.*

with variety, can obtain from Him whatever she will. Let us also seek the suffrages of the most blessed Peter, Prince of the Apostles, and of Paul his fellow apostle, and of all the saints in heaven, who, having now become God's friends, have arrived at the heavenly kingdom, and being crowned bear their palms, and, being secure of their own immortality, are anxious for our salvation.

12. Lastly, imploring from Our heart for you from God the abundance of all heavenly gifts, We most lovingly impart the Apostolic Benediction from Our inmost heart, a pledge of our signal love toward you, to yourselves, Venerable Brethren, and to all the clerics and lay faithful committed to your care.

Given at Rome, from St. Peter's, the eighth day of December, in the year 1864, the tenth from the dogmatic definition of the Immaculate Conception of the Virgin Mary, Mother of God.

In the nineteenth year of Our Pontificate.

Syllabus of Errors

ISSUED TOGETHER WITH QUANTA CURA

Pope Pius IX

December 8, 1864

Syllabus Embracing the Principal Errors of Our Time Which Are Censured in Consistorial Allocutions, Encyclicals, and Other Apostolic Letters of Our Most Holy Father, Pope Pius IX

I. PANTHEISM, NATURALISM, AND ABSOLUTE RATIONALISM

1. There exists no supreme, all-wise, all-provident divine Being, distinct from the universe, and God is identical with the nature of things, and is, therefore, subject to changes. In effect, God is produced in man and in the world, and all things are God and have the very substance of God, and God is one and the same thing with the world, and, therefore, spirit with matter, necessity with liberty, good with evil, justice with injustice.[33]

2. All action of God upon man and the world is to be denied.[34]

3. Human reason, without any reference whatsoever to God, is the sole arbiter of truth and falsehood, and of good and evil; it is law to itself, and suffices, by its natural force, to secure the welfare of men and of nations.[35]

[33] See Pope Pius IX, Allocution *Maxima quidem* (June 9, 1862).

[34] See Pope Pius IX, *Maxima quidem*.

[35] See Pope Pius IX, *Maxima quidem*.

4. All the truths of religion proceed from the innate strength of human reason; hence reason is the ultimate standard by which man can and ought to arrive at the knowledge of all truths of every kind.[36]

5. Divine revelation is imperfect, and therefore subject to a continual and indefinite progress, corresponding with the advancement of human reason.[37]

6. The faith of Christ is in opposition to human reason; and divine revelation not only is not useful, but is even hurtful to the perfection of man.[38]

7. The prophecies and miracles set forth and recorded in the Sacred Scriptures are the fiction of poets, and the mysteries of the Christian Faith the result of philosophical investigations. In the books of the Old and New Testament there are contained mythical inventions, and Jesus Christ is Himself a myth.[39]

II. MODERATE RATIONALISM

8. As human reason is placed on a level with religion itself, so theological must be treated in the same manner as philosophical sciences.[40]

9. All the dogmas of the Christian religion are indiscriminately the object of natural science or philosophy, and human reason, enlightened solely in a historical way, is able, by its own natural strength and principles, to attain to the true science of even the most ab-

[36] See Pope Pius IX, *Maxima quidem*; Encyclical *Qui pluribus* (November 9, 1846); and Encyclical *Singulari quidem* (March 17, 1856).

[37] See Pope Pius IX, *Maxima quidem*; and *Qui pluribus*.

[38] See Pope Pius IX, *Qui pluribus*; and *Maxima quidem*.

[39] See Pope Pius IX, *Maxima quidem*; and *Qui pluribus*.

[40] See Pope Pius IX, Allocution *Singulari quadam* (December 9, 1854).

struse dogmas; provided only that such dogmas be proposed to reason itself as its object.[41]

10. As the philosopher is one thing, and philosophy another, so it is the right and duty of the philosopher to subject himself to the authority which he shall have proved to be true; but philosophy neither can nor ought to submit to any such authority.[42]

11. The Church not only ought never to pass judgment on philosophy, but ought to tolerate the errors of philosophy, leaving it to correct itself.[43]

12. The decrees of the Apostolic See and of the Roman congregations impede the true progress of science.[44]

13. The method and principles by which the old scholastic doctors cultivated theology are no longer suitable to the demands of our times and to the progress of the sciences.[45]

14. Philosophy is to be treated without taking any account of supernatural revelation.[46]

41 See Pope Pius IX, Apostolic Letter *Gravissimas inter* (December 11, 1862); and Letter *Tuas libenter* (December 21, 1863).

42 See Pope Pius IX, *Gravissimas inter*; and *Tuas libenter*.

43 See Pope Pius IX, *Gravissimas inter*.

44 See Pope Pius IX, *Tuas libenter*.

45 See Pope Pius IX, *Tuas libenter*.

46 See Pope Pius IX, Apostolic Letter *Eximiam tuam* (June 15, 1857); Apostolic Letter *Dolore haud mediocri* (April 30, 1860); and *Tuas libenter*. N.B.: The errors of Antonius Günther, which are condemned in the Epistle to the Cardinal Archbishop of Cologne, *Eximiam tuam* (June 15, 1857), and in the Epistle to the Bishop of Wrocław, *Dolore haud mediocri* (April 30, 1860), are largely consistent with the system of rationalism.

III. INDIFFERENTISM, LATITUDINARIANISM

15. Every man is free to embrace and profess that religion which, guided by the light of reason, he shall consider true.[47]

16. Man may, in the observance of any religion whatever, find the way of eternal salvation, and arrive at eternal salvation.[48]

17. Good hope at least is to be entertained of the eternal salvation of all those who are not at all in the true Church of Christ.[49]

18. Protestantism is nothing more than another form of the same true Christian religion, in which form it is given to please God equally as in the Catholic Church.[50]

IV. SOCIALISM, COMMUNISM, SECRET SOCIETIES, BIBLICAL SOCIETIES, CLERICO-LIBERAL SOCIETIES

Pests of this kind are frequently reprobated in the severest terms in the Encyclical *Qui pluribus* (November 9, 1846), Allocution *Quibus quantisque* (April 20, 1849), Encyclical *Nostis et Nobiscum* (December 8, 1849), Allocution *Singulari quadam* (December 9, 1854), and Encyclical *Quanto conficiamur moerore* (August 10, 1863).

V. ERRORS CONCERNING THE CHURCH AND HER RIGHTS

19. The Church is not a true and perfect society, entirely free; nor is she endowed with proper and perpetual rights of her own, conferred upon her by her divine Founder; but it appertains to the civil

[47] See Pope Pius IX, Condemnation *Multiplices inter* (June 10, 1851); and *Maxima quidem*.

[48] See Pope Pius IX, Allocution *Ubi primum* (December 17, 1847); and Encyclical *Singulari quidem*.

[49] See Pope Pius IX, *Singulari quadam*; and Encyclical *Quanto conficiamur moerore* (August 10, 1863).

[50] See Pope Pius IX, Encyclical *Nostis et Nobiscum* (December 8, 1849).

power to define what are the rights of the Church, and the limits within which she may exercise those rights.[51]

20. The ecclesiastical power ought not to exercise its authority without the permission and assent of the civil government.[52]

21. The Church has not the power of defining dogmatically that the religion of the Catholic Church is the only true religion.[53]

22. The obligation by which Catholic teachers and authors are strictly bound is confined to those things only which are proposed to universal belief as dogmas of faith by the infallible judgment of the Church.[54]

23. Roman Pontiffs and ecumenical councils have wandered outside the limits of their powers, have usurped the rights of princes, and have even erred in defining matters of faith and morals.[55]

24. The Church has not the power of using force, nor has she any temporal power, direct or indirect.[56]

25. Besides the power inherent in the episcopate, other temporal power has been attributed to it by the civil authority granted either explicitly or tacitly, which on that account is revocable by the civil authority whenever it thinks fit.[57]

[51] See Pope Pius IX, *Singulari quadam*; Allocution *Novos et ante* (September 28, 1860); and *Maxima quidem*.
[52] See Pope Pius IX, Allocution *Meminit unusquisque* (September 30, 1861).
[53] See Pope Pius IX, *Multiplices inter* (June 10, 1851).
[54] See Pope Pius IX, *Tuas libenter*.
[55] See Pope Pius IX, *Multiplices inter* (June 10, 1851).
[56] See Pope Pius IX, Condemnation *Ad apostolicae* (August 22, 1851).
[57] See Pope Pius IX, *Ad apostolicae*.

26. The Church has no innate and legitimate right of acquiring and possessing property.[58]

27. The sacred ministers of the Church and the Roman Pontiff are to be absolutely excluded from every charge and dominion over temporal affairs.[59]

28. It is not lawful for bishops to publish even letters apostolic without the permission of government.[60]

29. Favors granted by the Roman Pontiff ought to be considered null, unless they have been sought for through the civil government.[61]

30. The immunity of the Church and of ecclesiastical persons derived its origin from civil law.[62]

31. The ecclesiastical forum or tribunal for the temporal causes, whether civil or criminal, of clerics ought by all means to be abolished, even without consulting and against the protest of the Holy See.[63]

32. The personal immunity by which clerics are exonerated from military conscription and service in the army may be abolished without violation either of natural right or equity. Its abolition is called for by civil progress, especially in a society framed on the model of a liberal government.[64]

[58] See Pope Pius IX, Allocution *Nunquam fore* (December 15, 1856); and Encyclical *Incredibili afflictamur* (September 17, 1863).
[59] See Pope Pius IX, *Maxima quidem.*
[60] See Pope Pius IX, *Nunquam fore.*
[61] See Pope Pius IX, *Nunquam fore.*
[62] See Pope Pius IX, *Multiplices inter* (June 10, 1851).
[63] See Pope Pius IX, Allocution *Acerbissimum* (September 27, 1852); and *Nunquam fore.*
[64] See Pope Pius IX, Letter *Singularis nobisque* (September 29, 1864).

33. It does not appertain exclusively to the power of ecclesiastical jurisdiction by right, proper and innate, to direct the teaching of theological questions.[65]

34. The teaching of those who compare the Sovereign Pontiff to a prince, free and acting in the universal Church, is a doctrine which prevailed in the Middle Ages.[66]

35. There is nothing to prevent the decree of a general council, or the act of all peoples, from transferring the supreme pontificate from the bishop and city of Rome to another bishop and another city.[67]

36. The definition of a national council does not admit of any subsequent discussion, and the civil authority can assume this principle as the basis of its acts.[68]

37. National churches, withdrawn from the authority of the Roman Pontiff and altogether separated, can be established.[69]

38. The Roman Pontiffs have, by their too arbitrary conduct, contributed to the division of the Church into Eastern and Western.[70]

VI. ERRORS ABOUT CIVIL SOCIETY, CONSIDERED BOTH IN ITSELF AND IN ITS RELATION TO THE CHURCH

39. The State, as being the origin and source of all rights, is endowed with a certain right not circumscribed by any limits.[71]

65 See Pope Pius IX, *Tuas libenter*.
66 See Pope Pius IX, *Ad apostolicae*.
67 See Pope Pius IX, *Ad apostolicae*.
68 See Pope Pius IX, *Ad apostolicae*.
69 See Pope Pius IX, Allocution *Multis gravibusque* (December 17, 1860); and Allocution *Iamdudum cernimus* (March 18, 1861).
70 See Pope Pius IX, *Ad apostolicae*.
71 See Pope Pius IX, *Maxima quidem*.

40. The teaching of the Catholic Church is hostile to the well-being and interests of society.[72]

41. The civil government, even when in the hands of an infidel sovereign, has a right to an indirect negative power over religious affairs. It therefore possesses not only the right called that of *exsequatur*, but also that of appeal, called *appellatio ab abusu*.[73]

42. In the case of conflicting laws enacted by the two powers, the civil law prevails.[74]

43. The secular power has authority to rescind, declare, and render null, solemn conventions, commonly called concordats, entered into with the Apostolic See, regarding the use of rights appertaining to ecclesiastical immunity, without the consent of the Apostolic See, and even in spite of its protest.[75]

44. The civil authority may interfere in matters relating to religion, morality, and spiritual government: hence, it can pass judgment on the instructions issued for the guidance of consciences, conformably with their mission, by the pastors of the Church. Further, it has the right to make enactments regarding the administration of the divine sacraments, and the dispositions necessary for receiving them.[76]

45. The entire government of public schools in which the youth of a Christian state is educated, except (to a certain extent) in the case of episcopal seminaries, may and ought to appertain to the civil

[72] See Pope Pius IX, Allocution *Quibus, quantisque* (April 20, 1849).
[73] See Pope Pius IX, *Ad apostolicae*.
[74] See Pope Pius IX, *Ad apostolicae*.
[75] See Pope Pius IX, Allocution *In consistoriali* (November 1, 1850); and *Multis gravibusque*.
[76] See Pope Pius IX, *Maxima quidem*.

power, and belong to it so far that no other authority whatsoever shall be recognized as having any right to interfere in the discipline of the schools, the arrangement of the studies, the conferring of degrees, in the choice or approval of the teachers.[77]

46. Moreover, even in ecclesiastical seminaries, the method of studies to be adopted is subject to the civil authority.[78]

47. The best theory of civil society requires that popular schools open to children of every class of the people, and, generally, all public institutes intended for instruction in letters and philosophical sciences and for carrying on the education of youth, should be freed from all ecclesiastical authority, control, and interference, and should be fully subjected to the civil and political power at the pleasure of the rulers, and according to the standard of the prevalent opinions of the age.[79]

48. Catholics may approve of the system of educating youth unconnected with Catholic Faith and the power of the Church, and which regards the knowledge of merely natural things, and only, or at least primarily, the ends of earthly social life.[80]

49. The civil power may prevent the prelates of the Church and the faithful from communicating freely and mutually with the Roman Pontiff.[81]

50. Lay authority possesses of itself the right of presenting bishops, and may require of them to undertake the administration of the diocese

77 See Pope Pius IX, *In consistoriali*; and Allocution *Quibus luctuosissimis* (September 5, 1851).

78 See Pope Pius IX, *Nunquam fore*.

79 See Pope Pius IX, Letter *Quum non sine* (July 14, 1864).

80 See Pope Pius IX, *Quum non sine*.

81 See Pope Pius IX, *Maxima quidem*.

before they receive canonical institution, and the letters apostolic from the Holy See.[82]

51. And, further, the lay government has the right of deposing bishops from their pastoral functions, and is not bound to obey the Roman Pontiff in those things which relate to the institution of bishoprics and the appointment of bishops.[83]

52. Government can, by its own right, alter the age prescribed by the Church for the religious profession of women and men; and may require of all religious orders to admit no person to take solemn vows without its permission.[84]

53. The laws enacted for the protection of religious orders and regarding their rights and duties ought to be abolished; nay, more, civil government may lend its assistance to all who desire to renounce the obligation which they have undertaken of a religious life, and to break their vows. Government may also suppress the said religious orders, as likewise collegiate churches and simple benefices, even those of advowson and subject their property and revenues to the administration and pleasure of the civil power.[85]

54. Kings and princes are not only exempt from the jurisdiction of the Church, but are superior to the Church in deciding questions of jurisdiction.[86]

55. The Church ought to be separated from the State, and the State from the Church.[87]

[82] See Pope Pius IX, *Nunquam fore.*

[83] See Pope Pius IX, *Multiplices inter* (June 10, 1851); and *Acerbissimum.*

[84] See Pope Pius IX, Allocution *Probe memineritis* (January 22, 1855); and *Nunquam fore.*

[85] See Pope Pius IX, *Acerbissimum*; and Allocution *Cum saepe* (July 26, 1855).

[86] See Pope Pius IX, *Multiplices inter* (June 10, 1851).

[87] See Pope Pius IX, *Acerbissimum.*

VII. ERRORS CONCERNING NATURAL AND CHRISTIAN ETHICS

56. Moral laws do not stand in need of the divine sanction, and it is not at all necessary that human laws should be made conformable to the laws of nature and receive their power of binding from God.[88]

57. The science of philosophical things and morals and also civil laws may and ought to keep aloof from divine and ecclesiastical authority.[89]

58. No other forces are to be recognized except those which reside in matter, and all the rectitude and excellence of morality ought to be placed in the accumulation and increase of riches by every possible means, and the gratification of pleasure.[90]

59. Right consists in the material fact. All human duties are an empty word, and all human facts have the force of right.[91]

60. Authority is nothing else but numbers and the sum total of material forces.[92]

61. The injustice of an act when successful inflicts no injury on the sanctity of right.[93]

62. The principle of non-intervention, as it is called, ought to be proclaimed and observed.[94]

63. It is lawful to refuse obedience to legitimate princes, and even to rebel against them.[95]

[88] See Pope Pius IX, *Maxima quidem*.
[89] See Pope Pius IX, *Maxima quidem*.
[90] See Pope Pius IX, *Maxima quidem*; and *Quanto conficiamur moerore*.
[91] See Pope Pius IX, *Maxima quidem*.
[92] See Pope Pius IX, *Maxima quidem*.
[93] See Pope Pius IX, *Iamdudum cernimus*.
[94] See Pope Pius IX, *Novos et ante*.
[95] See Pope Pius IX, *Qui pluribus*; Allocution *Quisque vestrum* (October 4, 1847); *Nostis et Nobiscum*; and Brief *Cum catholica Ecclesia* (March 26, 1860).

64. The violation of any solemn oath, as well as any wicked and flagitious action repugnant to the eternal law, is not only not blamable but is altogether lawful and worthy of the highest praise when done through love of country.[96]

VIII. ERRORS CONCERNING CHRISTIAN MARRIAGE

65. The doctrine that Christ has raised marriage to the dignity of a sacrament cannot be at all tolerated.[97]

66. The sacrament of marriage is only something accessory to the contract and separate from it, and the sacrament itself consists in the nuptial benediction alone.[98]

67. By the law of nature, the marriage tie is not indissoluble, and in many cases divorce properly so called may be decreed by the civil authority.[99]

68. The Church has not the power of establishing diriment impediments of marriage, but such a power belongs to the civil authority by which existing impediments are to be removed.[100]

69. In the dark ages the Church began to establish diriment impediments, not by her own right, but by using a power borrowed from the State.[101]

70. The canons of the Council of Trent, which anathematize those who dare to deny to the Church the right of establishing diriment

[96] See Pope Pius IX, Allocution *Quibus quantisque* (April 20, 1849).
[97] See Pope Pius IX, *Ad apostolicae.*
[98] See Pope Pius IX, *Ad apostolicae.*
[99] See Pope Pius IX, *Ad apostolicae*; and *Acerbissimum.*
[100] See Pope Pius IX, *Multiplices inter* (June 10, 1851).
[101] See Pope Pius IX, *Ad apostolicae.*

impediments, either are not dogmatic or must be understood as referring to such borrowed power.[102]

71. The form of solemnizing marriage prescribed by the Council of Trent, under pain of nullity, does not bind in cases where the civil law lays down another form, and declares that when this new form is used the marriage shall be valid.[103]

72. Boniface VIII was the first who declared that the vow of chastity taken at ordination renders marriage void.[104]

73. In force of a merely civil contract there may exist between Christians a real marriage, and it is false to say either that the marriage contract between Christians is always a sacrament, or that there is no contract if the sacrament be excluded.[105]

74. Matrimonial causes and espousals belong by their nature to civil tribunals.[106]

IX. ERRORS REGARDING THE CIVIL POWER OF THE SOVEREIGN PONTIFF

75. The children of the Christian and Catholic Church are divided amongst themselves about the compatibility of the temporal with the spiritual power.[107]

[102] See Pope Pius IX, *Ad apostolicae*.

[103] See Pope Pius IX, *Ad apostolicae*.

[104] See Pope Pius IX, *Ad apostolicae*.

[105] See Pope Pius IX, *Ad apostolicae*; Letter to the King of Sardinia (September 9, 1852); *Acerbissimum*; and *Multis gravibusque*.

[106] See Pope Pius IX, *Ad apostolicae*; and *Acerbissimum*. N. B.: We note two other errors here: abolishing the celibacy of clerics, and preferring the state of marriage to the state of virginity. The former is opposed in the Encyclical Letter *Qui pluribus* (November 9, 1846), the latter in the Apostolic Letter *Multiplices inter* (June 10, 1851).

[107] See Pope Pius IX, *Ad apostolicae*.

76. The abolition of the temporal power of which the Apostolic See is possessed would contribute in the greatest degree to the liberty and prosperity of the Church.[108]

X. ERRORS HAVING REFERENCE TO MODERN LIBERALISM

77. In the present day it is no longer expedient that the Catholic religion should be held as the only religion of the State, to the exclusion of all other forms of worship.[109]

78. Hence it has been wisely decided by law, in some Catholic countries, that persons coming to reside therein shall enjoy the public exercise of their own peculiar worship.[110]

79. Moreover, it is false that the civil liberty of every form of worship, and the full power, given to all, of overtly and publicly manifesting any opinions whatsoever and thoughts, conduce more easily to corrupt the morals and minds of the people, and to propagate the pest of indifferentism.[111]

80. The Roman Pontiff can, and ought to, reconcile himself, and come to terms with progress, liberalism, and modern civilization.[112]

[108] See Pope Pius IX, *Quibus quantisque*; Allocution *Si semper antea* (May 20, 1850); *Cum catholica Ecclesia*; *Novos et ante*; *Multis gravibusque*; *Iamdudum cernimus*; and *Maxima quidem*.

[109] See Pope Pius IX, Allocution *Nemo vestrum* (July 26, 1855).

[110] See Pope Pius IX, *Acerbissimum*.

[111] See Pope Pius IX, *Nunquam fore*.

[112] See Pope Pius IX, *Iamdudum cernimus*.

Spectata Fides

ENCYCLICAL ON CHRISTIAN EDUCATION

Pope Leo XIII

November 27, 1885

To Our Venerable Brethren, Henry Edward, Cardinal Priest of the Holy Roman Church, of the Title of Sts. Andrew and Gregory on the Coelian Hill, Archbishop of Westminster, and the other Bishops of England. Venerable Brethren, Health and Apostolic Benediction.

1. Your proved fidelity and singular devotion to this Apostolic See are admirably shown in the letter which We have lately received from you. Our pleasure in receiving it is indeed increased by the further knowledge which it gives Us of your great vigilance and anxiety, in a matter where no care can be too great: We mean the Christian education of your children, upon which you have lately taken counsel together, and have reported to us the decisions to which you came.

2. In this work of so great moment, Venerable Brethren, We rejoice much to see that you do not work alone; for We know how much is due to the whole body of your clergy. With the greatest charity, and with unconquered efforts, they have provided schools for their children; and, with wonderful diligence and assiduity, they endeavor by their teaching to form them to a Christian life, and to instruct them in the elements of knowledge. Wherefore, with all the encouragement and praise that Our voice can give, We bid your clergy to go on in their meritorious work, and to be assured of Our special commendation and good will, looking forward to

a far greater reward from Our Lord God for Whose sake they are laboring.

3. Not less worthy of commendation is the generosity of Catholics in this matter. We know how readily they supply what is needed for the maintenance of schools; not only those who are wealthy, but those also who are of slender means, and poor; and it is beautiful to see how, often from the earnings of their poverty, they willingly contribute to the education of children.

4. In these days, and in the present condition of the world, when the tender age of childhood is threatened on every side by so many and such various dangers, hardly anything can be imagined more fitting than the union with literary instruction of sound teaching in faith and morals. For this reason, We have more than once said that We strongly approve of the voluntary schools, which, by the work and liberality of private individuals, have been established in France, in Belgium, in America, and in the colonies of the British Empire. We desire their increase, as much as possible, and that they may flourish in the number of their scholars. We Ourselves also, seeing the condition of things in this city, continue, with the greatest effort and at great cost, to provide an abundance of such schools for the children of Rome. For it is in and by these schools that the Catholic Faith, our greatest and best inheritance, is preserved whole and entire. In these schools, the liberty of parents is respected; and, what is most needed, especially in the prevailing license of opinion and of action, it is by these schools that good citizens are brought up for the State; for there is no better citizen than the man who has believed and practiced the Christian Faith from his childhood. The beginning and, as it were, the seed of that human perfection which Jesus Christ gave to mankind are to be found in the Christian education of the young; for the future condition of the State depends upon the early training of its children. The wisdom of our forefathers, and the very foundations of the

State, are ruined by the destructive error of those who would have children brought up without religious education. You see, therefore Venerable Brethren, with what earnest forethought parents must beware of entrusting their children to schools in which they cannot receive religious teaching.

5. In your country of Great Britain, We know that, besides yourselves, very many of your nation are not a little anxious about religious education. They do not in all things agree with Us; nevertheless, they see how important, for the sake both of society and of men individually, is the preservation of that Christian wisdom which your forefathers received through St. Augustine, from Our predecessor, Gregory the Great: which wisdom the violent tempests that came afterward have not entirely scattered. There are, as We know, at this day, many of an excellent disposition of mind, who are diligently striving to retain what they can of the ancient Faith, and who bring forth many and great fruits of charity. As often as We think of this, so often are we deeply moved, for We love with a paternal charity that island which was not undeservedly called the Mother of Saints; and We see, in the disposition of mind of which We have spoken, the greatest hope and, as it were, a pledge of the welfare and prosperity of the British people. Go on, therefore, Venerable Brethren, in making the young your chief care; press onward in every way your episcopal work; and cultivate with alacrity and hopefulness whatever good seeds you find: for God, Who is rich in mercy, will give the increase.

6. As a pledge of gifts from above, and in witness of Our good will, We lovingly grant in the Lord to you, and to the clergy and people commited to each one of you, the Apostolic Benediction.

Given at Rome, at St. Peter's, on the twenty-seventh day of November, in the year 1885, the eighth year of Our Pontificate.

Acerbo Nimis

ENCYCLICAL ON TEACHING CHRISTIAN DOCTRINE

Pope Pius X

April 15, 1905

To the Patriarchs, Primates, Archbishops, Bishops, and other Ordinaries in Peace and Communion with the Apostolic See. Venerable Brethren, Health and the Apostolic Blessing.

Ignorance Breeds Indifference

1. At this very troublesome and difficult time, the hidden designs of God have conducted Our poor strength to the office of Supreme Pastor, to rule the entire flock of Christ. The enemy has, indeed, long been prowling about the fold and attacking it with such subtle cunning that now, more than ever before, the prediction of the apostle to the elders of the Church of Ephesus seems to be verified: "I know that … fierce wolves will get in among you, and will not spare the flock" (Acts 20:29). Those who still are zealous for the glory of God are seeking the causes and reasons for this decline in religion. Coming to a different explanation, each points out, according to his own view, a different plan for the protection and restoration of the Kingdom of God on earth. But it seems to Us, Venerable Brethren, that while we should not overlook other considerations, We are forced to agree with those who hold that the chief cause of the present indifference and, as it were, infirmity of soul, and the serious evils that result from it, is to be found above all in ignorance of things divine. This is fully in accord with what God Himself declared through the prophet Osee: "And there is no knowledge of God in the land. Cursing and lying and killing and theft and adultery have overflowed: and blood hath touched blood.

Thereafter shall the land mourn, and everyone that dwelleth in it shall languish" (Os 4:1–3).

Effects of Religious Ignorance

2. It is a common complaint, unfortunately too well founded, that there are large numbers of Christians in our own time who are entirely ignorant of those truths necessary for salvation. And when we mention Christians, We refer not only to the masses or to those in the lower walks of life—for these find some excuse for their ignorance in the fact that the demands of their harsh employers hardly leave them time to take care of themselves or of their dear ones—but We refer to those especially who do not lack culture or talents and, indeed, are possessed of abundant knowledge regarding things of the world, but live rashly and imprudently with regard to religion. It is hard to find words to describe how profound is the darkness in which they are engulfed and, what is most deplorable of all, how tranquilly they repose there. They rarely give thought to God, the Supreme Author and Ruler of all things, or to the teachings of the Faith of Christ. They know nothing of the Incarnation of the Word of God, nothing of the perfect restoration of the human race which He accomplished. Grace, the greatest of the helps for attaining eternal things, the Holy Sacrifice and the sacraments by which we obtain grace, are entirely unknown to them. They have no conception of the malice and baseness of sin; hence they show no anxiety to avoid sin or to renounce it. And so they arrive at life's end in such a condition that, lest all hope of salvation be lost, the priest is obliged to give in the last few moments of life a summary teaching of religion, a time which should be devoted to stimulating the soul to greater love for God. And even this as too often happens only when the dying man is not so sinfully ignorant as to look upon the ministration of the priest as useless, and then calmly faces the fearful passage to eternity without making his peace with God. And so Our predecessor, Benedict XIV, had just

cause to write: "We declare that a great number of those who are condemned to eternal punishment suffer that everlasting calamity because of ignorance of those mysteries of faith which must be known and believed in order to be numbered among the elect."[113]

Intellect is the Guide to Holiness

3. There is then, Venerable Brethren, no reason for wonder that the corruption of morals and depravity of life is already so great, and ever increasingly greater, not only among uncivilized peoples but even in those very nations that are called Christian. The apostle Paul, writing to the Ephesians, repeatedly admonished them in these words: "But immorality and every uncleanness or covetousness, let it not even be named among you, as become saints; or obscenity or foolish talk" (5:3–4). He also places the foundation of holiness and sound morals upon a knowledge of divine things—which holds in check evil desires: "See to it therefore, brethren, that you walk with care: not as unwise but as wise.... Therefore, do not become foolish, but understand what the will of the Lord is" (Eph 5:15–17). And rightly so. For the will of man retains but little of that divinely implanted love of virtue and righteousness by which it was, as it were, attracted strongly toward the real and not merely apparent good. Disordered by the stain of the first sin, and almost forgetful of God, its Author, it improperly turns every affection to a love of vanity and deceit. This erring will, blinded by its own evil desires, has need therefore of a guide to lead it back to the paths of justice whence it has so unfortunately strayed. The intellect itself is this guide, which need not be sought elsewhere, but is provided by nature itself. It is a guide, though, that, if it lack its companion light, the knowledge of divine things, will be only an instance of the blind leading the blind so that both will fall into the pit. The holy king David, praising God for the light of truth with which He had illumined the intellect, exclaimed: "The light of Thy countenance,

[113] *Institutiones Ecclesiasticae*, 27:18.

O Lord, is signed upon us" (Ps 4:7). Then he described the effect of this light by adding: "Thou hast given gladness in my heart" (Ps 4:7), gladness, that is, which enlarges our heart so that it runs in the way of God's commandments.

Christian Doctrine Enlightens the Intellect

4. All this becomes evident on a little reflection. Christian teaching reveals God and His infinite perfection with far greater clarity than is possible by the human faculties alone. Nor is that all. This same Christian teaching also commands us to honor God by faith, which is of the mind, by hope, which is of the will, by love, which is of the heart; and thus the whole man is subjected to the supreme Maker and Ruler of all things. The truly remarkable dignity of man as the son of the heavenly Father, in Whose image he is formed, and with Whom he is destined to live in eternal happiness, is also revealed only by the doctrine of Jesus Christ. From this very dignity, and from man's knowledge of it, Christ showed that men should love one another as brothers, and should live here as become children of light, "not of revelry and drunkenness, not in debauchery and wantonness, not in strife and jealousy" (Rom 13:13). He also bids us to place all our anxiety and care in the hands of God, for He will provide for us; He tells us to help the poor, to do good to those who hate us, and to prefer the eternal welfare of the soul to the temporal goods of this life. Without wishing to touch on every detail, nevertheless, is it not true that the proud man is urged and commanded by the teaching of Christ to strive for humility, the source of true glory? "Whoever, therefore, humbles himself … he is the greatest in the kingdom of heaven" (Mt 18:4). From that same teaching we learn prudence of the spirit, and thereby we avoid prudence of the flesh; we learn justice, by which we give to every man his due; fortitude, which prepares us to endure all things and with steadfast heart suffer all things for the sake of God and eternal happiness; and, last of all, temperance through which we cherish even poverty

borne out of love for God, nay, we even glory in the cross itself, unmindful of its shame. In fine, Christian teaching not only bestows on the intellect the light by which it attains truth, but from it our will draws that ardor by which we are raised up to God and joined with Him in the practice of virtue.

Intellect Moves the Will to Action

5. We by no means wish to conclude that a perverse will and unbridled conduct may not be joined with a knowledge of religion. Would to God that facts did not too abundantly prove the contrary! But We do maintain that the will cannot be upright nor the conduct good when the mind is shrouded in the darkness of crass ignorance. A man who walks with open eyes may, indeed, turn aside from the right path, but a blind man is in much more imminent danger of wandering away. Furthermore, there is always some hope for a reform of perverse conduct so long as the light of faith is not entirely extinguished; but if lack of faith is added to depraved morality because of ignorance, the evil hardly admits of remedy, and the road to ruin lies open.

Christian Living Follows Christian Doctrine

6. How many and how grave are the consequences of ignorance in matters of religion! And on the other hand, how necessary and how beneficial is religious instruction! It is indeed vain to expect a fulfillment of the duties of a Christian by one who does not even know them.

Duty of Pastors

7. We must now consider upon whom rests the obligation to dissipate this most pernicious ignorance and to impart in its stead the knowledge that is wholly indispensable. There can be no doubt, Venerable Brethren, that this most important duty rests upon all who are pastors of souls. On them, by command of Christ, rest the

obligations of knowing and of feeding the flocks committed to their care; and "to feed" implies, first of all, to teach. "I will give you pastors according to My own heart," God promised through Jeremias, "and they shall feed you with knowledge and doctrine" (Jer 3:15). Hence the apostle Paul said: "Christ did not send me to baptize, but to preach the gospel" (1 Cor 1:17), thereby indicating that the first duty of all those who are entrusted in any way with the government of the Church is to instruct the faithful in the things of God.

Dignity of the Teacher

8. We do not think it necessary to set forth here the praises of such instruction or to point out how meritorious it is in God's sight. If, assuredly, the alms with which we relieve the needs of the poor are highly praised by the Lord, how much more precious in His eyes, then, will be the zeal and labor expended in teaching and admonishing, by which we provide not for the passing needs of the body but for the eternal profit of the soul! Nothing, surely, is more desirable, nothing more acceptable to Jesus Christ, the Savior of souls, Who testifies of Himself through Isaias: "To bring good news to the poor He has sent Me" (Lk 4:18).

Priestly Holiness and Learning

9. Here then it is well to emphasize and insist that for a priest there is no duty more grave or obligation more binding than this. Who, indeed, will deny that knowledge should be joined to holiness of life in the priest? "For the lips of the priest shall keep knowledge" (Mal 2:7). The Church demands this knowledge of those who are to be ordained to the priesthood. Why? Because the Christian people expect from them knowledge of the divine law, and it was for that end that they were sent by God. "And they shall seek the law at his mouth; because he is the angel of the Lord of hosts" (Mal 2:7). Thus the bishop speaking to the candidates for the priesthood in the ordination ceremony says: "Let your teaching be a spiritual

remedy for God's people; may they be worthy fellow workers of our order; and thus meditating day and night on His law, they may believe what they read, and teach what they shall believe."[114]

Parish Priests Must Teach

10. If what We have just said is applicable to all priests, does it not apply with much greater force to those who possess the title and the authority of parish priests, and who, by virtue of their rank and in a sense by virtue of a contract, hold the office of pastors of souls? These are, to a certain extent, the pastors and teachers appointed by Christ in order that the faithful might not be as "children, tossed to and fro and carried about by every wind of doctrine devised in the wickedness of men," but that, practicing "the truth in love," they may "grow up in all things in Him Who is the head, Christ" (Eph 4:14–15).

Teaching is Their Primary Duty

11. For this reason, the Council of Trent, treating of the duties of pastors of souls, decreed that their first and most important work is the instruction of the faithful.[115] It therefore prescribes that they shall teach the truths of religion on Sundays and on the more solemn feast days;[116] moreover during the holy seasons of Advent and Lent they are to give such instruction every day or at least three times a week.[117] This, however, was not considered enough. The council provided for the instruction of youth by adding that the pastors, either personally or through others, must explain the truths of religion at least on Sundays and feast days to the children of the par-

[114] Roman Pontifical.

[115] See Session 5, *Decree on Reformation*, chap. 2.

[116] See Council of Trent, Session 5, *Decree on Reformation*, chap. 2; Session 22, *Doctrine on the Sacrifice of the Mass*, chap. 8; and Session 24, *Decree on Reformation*, chaps. 4, 7.

[117] See Council of Trent, Session 24, *Decree on Reformation*, chap. 4.

ish, and inculcate obedience to God and to their parents.[118] When the sacraments are to be administered, it enjoins upon pastors the duty to explain their efficacy in plain and simple language.[119]

Holiness and Instruction

12. These prescriptions of the Council of Trent have been summarized and still more clearly defined by Our predecessor, Benedict XIV, in his Constitution *Etsi minime*. "Two chief obligations," he wrote, "have been imposed by the Council of Trent on those who have the care of souls: first, that of preaching the things of God to the people on the feast days; and second, that of teaching the rudiments of faith and of the divine law to the youth and others who need such instruction." Here the wise pontiff rightly distinguishes between these two duties: one is what is commonly known as the explanation of the Gospel and the other is the teaching of Christian doctrine. Perhaps there are some who, wishing to lessen their labors, would believe that the homily on the Gospel can take the place of catechetical instruction. But for one who reflects a moment, such is obviously impossible. The sermon on the holy Gospel is addressed to those who should have already received knowledge of the elements of faith. It is, so to speak, bread broken for adults. Catechetical instruction, on the other hand, is that milk which the apostle Peter wished the faithful to desire in all simplicity like newborn babes (see 1 Pt 2:2).

The Task of the Catechist

13. The task of the catechist is to take up one or other of the truths of faith or of Christian morality and then explain it in all its parts; and since amendment of life is the chief aim of his instruction, the catechist must needs make a comparison between what God

[118] See Council of Trent, Session 24, *Decree on Reformation*, chap. 4.

[119] See Council of Trent, Session 22, *Doctrine on the Sacrifice of the Mass*, chap. 8; and Session 24, *Decree on Reformation*, chap. 7.

commands us to do and what is our actual conduct. After this, he will use examples appropriately taken from the Holy Scriptures, Church history, and the lives of the saints—thus moving his hearers and clearly pointing out to them how they are to regulate their own conduct. He should, in conclusion, earnestly exhort all present to dread and avoid vice and to practice virtue.

PRIMACY OF CATECHETICAL INSTRUCTION

14. We are indeed aware that the work of teaching the catechism is unpopular with many because, as a rule, it is deemed of little account, and for the reason that it does not lend itself easily to the winning of public praise. But this in Our opinion is a judgment based on vanity and devoid of truth. We do not disapprove of those pulpit orators who, out of genuine zeal for the glory of God, devote themselves to defense of the Faith and to its spread, or who eulogize the saints of God. But their labor presupposes labor of another kind, that of the catechist. And so, if this be lacking, then the foundation is wanting; and they labor in vain who build the house (see Ps 126:1). Too often it happens that ornate sermons which receive the applause of crowded congregations serve but to tickle the ears and fail utterly to touch the hearts of the hearers. Catechetical instruction, on the other hand, plain and simple though it be, is the word of which God Himself speaks through the lips of the prophet Isaias: "And as the rain and the snow come down from heaven, and return no more thither, but soak the earth and water it, and make it to spring and give seed to the sower and bread to the eater: so shall My Word be, which shall go forth from My mouth. It shall not return to Me void, but it shall do whatsoever I please and shall prosper in the things for which I sent it" (Is 55:10–11). We believe the same may be said of those priests who work hard to produce books which explain the truths of religion. They are surely to be commended for their zeal, but how many are there who read these works and take from them a fruit commensurate with the labor

and intention of the writers? The teaching of the catechism, on the other hand, when rightly done, never fails to profit those who listen to it.

Supernatural Motives for the Catechist

15. In order to enkindle the zeal of the ministers of God, We again insist on the need to reach the ever-increasing numbers of those who know nothing at all of religion, or who possess at most only such knowledge of God and Christian truths as befits idolaters. How many there are, alas, not only among the young, but among adults and those advanced in years, who know nothing of the chief mysteries of faith; who on hearing the name of Christ can only ask: "Who is He . . . that I may believe in Him?" (Jn 9:36). In consequence of this ignorance, they do not consider it a crime to excite and nourish hatred against their neighbor, to enter into most unjust contracts, to do business in dishonest fashion, to hold the funds of others at an exorbitant interest rate, and to commit other iniquities no less reprehensible. They are, moreover, ignorant of the law of Christ which not only condemns immoral actions but also forbids deliberate immoral thoughts and desires. Even when for some reason or other they avoid sensual pleasures, they nevertheless entertain evil thoughts without the least scruple, thereby multiplying their sins above the number of the hairs of the head. These persons are found, we deem it necessary to repeat, not merely among the poorer classes of the people or in sparsely settled districts, but also among those in the higher walks of life, even, indeed, among those puffed up with learning, who, relying upon a vain erudition, feel free to ridicule religion and to "deride whatever they do not know" (Jude 10).

God's Grace Demands Man's Cooperation

16. Now, if we cannot expect to reap a harvest when no seed has been planted, how can we hope to have a people with sound morals if

Christian doctrine has not been imparted to them in due time? It follows, too, that if faith languishes in our days, if among large numbers it has almost vanished, the reason is that the duty of catechetical teaching is either fulfilled very superficially or altogether neglected. It will not do to say, in excuse, that faith is a free gift of God bestowed upon each one at baptism. True enough, when we are baptized in Christ, the habit of faith is given, but this most divine seed, if left entirely to itself, by its own power, so to speak, is not like the mustard seed which "grows up ... and puts out great branches" (Mk 4:32). Man has the faculty of understanding at his birth, but he also has need of his mother's word to awaken it, as it were, and to make it active. So too, the Christian, born again of water and the Holy Spirit, has faith within him, but he requires the word of the teaching Church to nourish and develop it and to make it bear fruit. Thus wrote the apostle: "Faith then depends on hearing, and hearing on the word of Christ" (Rom 10:17); and to show the necessity of instruction, he added, "How are they to hear, if no one preaches?" (Rom 10:14).

Restore Catechetical Instruction

17. What We have said so far demonstrates the supreme importance of religious instruction. We ought, therefore, to do all that lies in our power to maintain the teaching of Christian doctrine with full vigor, and where such is neglected, to restore it; for, in the words of Our predecessor, Benedict XIV, "there is nothing more effective than catechetical instruction to spread the glory of God and to secure the salvation of souls."[120]

Regulations to Be Universally Observed

18. We, therefore, Venerable Brethren, desirous of fulfilling this most important obligation of Our teaching office, and likewise wishing to introduce uniformity everywhere in so weighty a matter, do by

[120] *Etsi minime*, no. 13.

Our supreme authority enact the following regulations and strictly command that they be observed and carried out in all dioceses of the world.

One Hour Weekly Instruction for Youth

19. I. On every Sunday and holy day, with no exception, throughout the year, all parish priests and in general all those having the care of souls shall instruct the boys and girls, for the space of an hour from the text of the catechism on those things they must believe and do in order to attain salvation.

Preparation for the Sacraments

20. II. At certain times throughout the year, they shall prepare boys and girls to receive properly the sacraments of penance and confirmation, by a continued instruction over a period of days.

Lenten Eucharistic Instruction

21. III. With a very special zeal, on every day in Lent and, if necessary, on the days following Easter, they shall instruct with the use of apt illustrations and exhortations the youth of both sexes to receive their First Communion in a holy manner.

The Confraternity of Christian Doctrine

22. IV. In each and every parish the society known as the Confraternity of Christian Doctrine is to be canonically established. Through this confraternity, the pastors, especially in places where there is a scarcity of priests, will have lay helpers in the teaching of the catechism, who will take up the work of imparting knowledge both from a zeal for the glory of God and in order to gain the numerous indulgences granted by the Sovereign Pontiffs.

Release-Time Religious Instruction

23. V. In the larger cities, and especially where universities, colleges, and secondary schools are located, let classes in religion be organized to instruct in the truths of faith and in the practice of Christian life the youths who attend the public schools from which all religious teaching is banned.

Adult Catechetical Instruction

24. VI. Since it is a fact that in these days adults need instruction no less than the young, all pastors and those having the care of souls shall explain the catechism to the people in a plain and simple style adapted to the intelligence of their hearers. This shall be carried out on all holy days of obligation, at such time as is most convenient for the people, but not during the same hour when the children are instructed, and this instruction must be in addition to the usual homily on the Gospel which is delivered at the parochial Mass on Sundays and holy days. The catechetical instruction shall be based on the Catechism of the Council of Trent; and the matter is to be divided in such a way that, in the space of four or five years, treatment will be given to the Apostles' Creed, the sacraments, the Ten Commandments, the Lord's Prayer, and the precepts of the Church.

Bishops Are to Carry Out These Regulations

25. Venerable Brethren, We decree and command this by virtue of Our Apostolic authority. It now rests with you to put it into prompt and complete execution in your respective dioceses, and by the power of your authority to see to it that these prescriptions of Ours be not neglected or, what amounts to the same thing, that they be not carried out carelessly or superficially. That this may be avoided, you must exhort and urge your pastors not to impart these instructions without having first prepared themselves in the work. Then they will not merely speak words of human wisdom, but "in simplicity

and godly sincerity" (2 Cor 1:12), imitating the example of Jesus Christ, Who, though He revealed "things hidden since the foundation of the world" (Mt 13:35), yet spoke "all ... things to the crowds in parables, and without parables ... did not speak to them" (Mt 13:34). We know that the apostles, who were taught by the Lord, did the same; for of them Pope St. Gregory wrote: "They took supreme care to preach to the uninstructed simple truths easy to understand, not things deep and difficult."[121] In matters of religion, the majority of men in our times must be considered uninstructed.

Necessity of Teacher's Preparation

26. We do not, however, wish to give the impression that this studied simplicity in imparting instruction does not require labor and meditation; on the contrary, it demands both, more than any other kind of preaching. It is much easier to find a preacher capable of delivering an eloquent and elaborate discourse than a catechist who can impart a catechetical instruction which is praiseworthy in every detail. No matter what natural facility a person may have in ideas and language, let him always remember that he will never be able to teach Christian doctrine to children or to adults without first giving himself to very careful study and preparation. They are mistaken who think that because of inexperience and lack of training of the people the work of catechizing can be performed in a slipshod fashion. On the contrary, the less educated the hearers, the more zeal and diligence must be used to adapt the sublime truths to their untrained minds; these truths, indeed, far surpass the natural understanding of the people, yet must be known by all—the uneducated and the cultured—in order that they may arrive at eternal happiness.

[121] *Moralia in Job*, vol. 2, pt. 4, bk. 17, chap. 26.

Plea for United Effort

27. And now, Venerable Brethren, permit Us to close this letter by addressing to you these words of Moses: "If any man be on the Lord's side, let him join with me" (Ex 32:26). We pray and entreat you to reflect on the great loss of souls due solely to ignorance of divine things. You have doubtless accomplished many useful and most praiseworthy works in your respective dioceses for the good of the flock entrusted to your care, but before all else, and with all possible zeal and diligence and care, see to it and urge on others that the knowledge of Christian doctrine pervades and imbues fully and deeply the minds of all. Here, using the words of the apostle Peter, We say, "According to the gift that each has received, administer it to one another as good stewards of the manifold grace of God" (1 Pt 4:10).

28. Through the intercession of the most Blessed Immaculate Virgin, may your diligent efforts be made fruitful by the Apostolic Blessing which, in token of Our affection and as a pledge of heavenly favors, We wholeheartedly impart to you and to your clergy and people.

Given at Rome, at St. Peter's, on the fifteenth day of April 1905, in the second year of Our Pontificate.

Lamentabili Sane

SYLLABUS CONDEMNING THE ERRORS OF THE MODERNISTS

Pope Pius X

July 3, 1907

With truly lamentable results, our age, casting aside all restraint in its search for the ultimate causes of things, frequently pursues novelties so ardently that it rejects the legacy of the human race. Thus it falls into very serious errors, which are even more serious when they concern sacred authority, the interpretation of Sacred Scripture, and the principal mysteries of Faith. The fact that many Catholic writers also go beyond the limits determined by the Fathers and the Church herself is extremely regrettable. In the name of higher knowledge and historical research (they say), they are looking for that progress of dogmas which is, in reality, nothing but the corruption of dogmas.

These errors are being daily spread among the faithful. Lest they captivate the faithful's minds and corrupt the purity of their faith, His Holiness, Pius X, by divine Providence, Pope, has decided that the chief errors should be noted and condemned by the Office of this Holy Roman and Universal Inquisition.

Therefore, after a very diligent investigation and consultation with the Reverend Consultors, the Most Eminent and Reverend Lord Cardinals, the General Inquisitors in matters of faith and morals have judged the following propositions to be condemned and proscribed. In fact, by this general decree, they are condemned and proscribed.

Errors regarding Scripture and Authority

1. The ecclesiastical law which prescribes that books concerning the divine Scriptures are subject to previous examination does not apply to critical scholars and students of scientific exegesis of the Old and New Testament.

2. The Church's interpretation of the Sacred Books is by no means to be rejected; nevertheless, it is subject to the more accurate judgment and correction of the exegetes.

3. From the ecclesiastical judgments and censures passed against free and more scientific exegesis, one can conclude that the Faith the Church proposes contradicts history and that Catholic teaching cannot really be reconciled with the true origins of the Christian religion.

4. Even by dogmatic definitions the Church's Magisterium cannot determine the genuine sense of the Sacred Scriptures.

5. Since the Deposit of Faith contains only revealed truths, the Church has no right to pass judgment on the assertions of the human sciences.

6. The "Church learning" and the "Church teaching" collaborate in such a way in defining truths that it only remains for the "Church teaching" to sanction the opinions of the "Church learning."

7. In proscribing errors, the Church cannot demand any internal assent from the faithful by which the judgments she issues are to be embraced.

8. They are free from all blame who treat lightly the condemnations passed by the Sacred Congregation of the Index or by the Roman Congregations.

9. They display excessive simplicity or ignorance who believe that God is really the Author of the Sacred Scriptures.

10. The inspiration of the books of the Old Testament consists in this: the Israelite writers handed down religious doctrines under a peculiar aspect which was either little or not at all known to the Gentiles.

11. Divine inspiration does not extend to all of Sacred Scriptures so that it renders its parts, each and every one, free from every error.

12. If he wishes to apply himself usefully to biblical studies, the exegete must first put aside all preconceived opinions about the supernatural origin of Sacred Scripture and interpret it the same as any other merely human document.

13. The evangelists themselves, as well as the Christians of the second and third generation, artificially arranged the evangelical parables. In such a way they explained the scanty fruit of the preaching of Christ among the Jews.

14. In many narrations the evangelists recorded, not so much things that are true, as things which, even though false, they judged to be more profitable for their readers.

15. Until the time the canon was defined and constituted, the Gospels were increased by additions and corrections. Therefore, there remained in them only a faint and uncertain trace of the doctrine of Christ.

16. The narrations of John are not properly history, but a mystical contemplation of the Gospel. The discourses contained in his Gospel are theological meditations, lacking historical truth concerning the mystery of salvation.

17. The fourth Gospel exaggerated miracles not only in order that the extraordinary might stand out but also in order that it might become more suitable for showing forth the work and glory of the Word incarnate.

18. John claims for himself the quality of witness concerning Christ. In reality, however, he is only a distinguished witness of the Christian life, or of the life of Christ in the Church at the close of the first century.

19. Heterodox exegetes have expressed the true sense of the Scriptures more faithfully than Catholic exegetes.

Errors regarding Divine Revelation

20. Revelation could be nothing else than the consciousness man acquired of his revelation to God.

21. Revelation, constituting the object of the Catholic faith, was not completed with the apostles.

22. The dogmas the Church holds out as revealed are not truths which have fallen from heaven. They are an interpretation of religious facts which the human mind has acquired by laborious effort.

23. Opposition may, and actually does, exist between the facts narrated in Sacred Scripture and the Church's dogmas which rest on them. Thus the critic may reject as false facts the Church holds as most certain.

24. The exegete who constructs premises from which it follows that dogmas are historically false or doubtful is not to be reproved as long as he does not directly deny the dogmas themselves.

25. The assent of faith ultimately rests on a mass of probabilities.

26. The dogmas of the Faith are to be held only according to their practical sense; that is to say, as preceptive norms of conduct and not as norms of believing.

ERRORS REGARDING THE SAVIOR

27. The divinity of Jesus Christ is not proved from the Gospels. It is a dogma which the Christian conscience has derived from the notion of the Messias.

28. While He was exercising His ministry, Jesus did not speak with the object of teaching He was the Messias, nor did His miracles tend to prove it.

29. It is permissible to grant that the Christ of history is far inferior to the Christ Who is the object of faith.

30. In all the evangelical texts, the name "Son of God" is equivalent only to that of "Messias." It does not in the least way signify that Christ is the true and natural Son of God.

31. The doctrine concerning Christ taught by Paul, John, and the Councils of Nicea, Ephesus, and Chalcedon is not that which Jesus taught but that which the Christian conscience conceived concerning Jesus.

32. It is impossible to reconcile the natural sense of the Gospel texts with the sense taught by our theologians concerning the conscience and the infallible knowledge of Jesus Christ.

33. Everyone who is not led by preconceived opinions can readily see that either Jesus professed an error concerning the immediate Messianic coming or the greater part of His doctrine as contained in the Gospels is destitute of authenticity.

34. The critics can ascribe to Christ a knowledge without limits only on a hypothesis which cannot be historically conceived and which is repugnant to the moral sense. That hypothesis is that Christ as man possessed the knowledge of God and yet was unwilling to communicate the knowledge of a great many things to His disciples and posterity.

35. Christ did not always possess the consciousness of His Messianic dignity.

36. The Resurrection of the Savior is not properly a fact of the historical order. It is a fact of merely the supernatural order (neither demonstrated nor demonstrable) which the Christian conscience gradually derived from other facts.

37. In the beginning, faith in the Resurrection of Christ was not so much in the fact itself of the Resurrection as in the immortal life of Christ with God.

38. The doctrine of the expiatory death of Christ is Pauline and not evangelical.

Errors regarding the Sacraments

39. The opinions concerning the origin of the sacraments which the Fathers of Trent held and which certainly influenced their dogmatic canons are very different from those which now rightly exist among historians who examine Christianity.

40. The sacraments have their origin in the fact that the apostles and their successors, swayed and moved by circumstances and events, interpreted some idea and intention of Christ.

41. The sacraments are intended merely to recall to man's mind the ever-beneficent presence of the Creator.

42. The Christian community imposed the necessity of baptism, adopted it as a necessary rite, and added to it the obligation of the Christian profession.

43. The practice of administering baptism to infants was a disciplinary evolution, which became one of the causes why the sacrament was divided into two, namely, baptism and penance.

44. There is nothing to prove that the rite of the sacrament of confirmation was employed by the apostles. The formal distinction of the two sacraments of baptism and confirmation does not pertain to the history of primitive Christianity.

45. Not everything which Paul narrates concerning the institution of the Eucharist (see 1 Cor 11:23–25) is to be taken historically.

46. In the primitive Church, the concept of the Christian sinner reconciled by the authority of the Church did not exist. Only very slowly did the Church accustom herself to this concept. As a matter of fact, even after penance was recognized as an institution of

the Church, it was not called a sacrament since it would be held as a disgraceful sacrament.

47. The words of the Lord, "Receive the Holy Spirit; whose sins you shall forgive, they are forgiven them; and whose sins you shall retain, they are retained" (Jn 20:22–23), in no way refer to the sacrament of penance, in spite of what it pleased the Fathers of Trent to say.

48. In his epistle (5:14–15), James did not intend to promulgate a sacrament of Christ but only commend a pious custom. If in this custom he happens to distinguish a means of grace, it is not in that rigorous manner in which it was taken by the theologians who laid down the notion and number of the sacraments.

49. When the Christian supper gradually assumed the nature of a liturgical action, those who customarily presided over the supper acquired the sacerdotal character.

50. The elders who fulfilled the office of watching over the gatherings of the faithful were instituted by the apostles as priests or bishops to provide for the necessary ordering of the increasing communities and not properly for the perpetuation of the apostolic mission and power.

51. It is impossible that matrimony could have become a sacrament of the New Law until later in the Church since it was necessary that a full theological explication of the doctrine of grace and the sacraments should first take place before matrimony should be held as a sacrament.

Errors regarding the Church

52. It was far from the mind of Christ to found a Church as a society which would continue on earth for a long course of centuries. On the contrary, in the mind of Christ, the kingdom of heaven together with the end of the world was about to come immediately.

53. The organic constitution of the Church is not immutable. Like human society, Christian society is subject to a perpetual evolution.

54. Dogmas, sacraments, and hierarchy, both their notion and reality, are only interpretations and evolutions of the Christian intelligence which have increased and perfected by an external series of additions the little germ latent in the Gospel.

55. Simon Peter never even suspected that Christ entrusted the primacy in the Church to him.

56. The Roman Church became the head of all the churches, not through the ordinance of divine Providence, but merely through political conditions.

57. The Church has shown that she is hostile to the progress of the natural and theological sciences.

58. Truth is no more immutable than man himself, since it evolved with him, in him, and through him.

59. Christ did not teach a determined body of doctrine applicable to all times and all men, but rather inaugurated a religious movement adapted or to be adapted to different times and places.

60. Christian doctrine was originally Judaic. Through successive evolutions it became first Pauline, then Joannine, finally Hellenic and universal.

61. It may be said without paradox that there is no chapter of Scripture, from the first of Genesis to the last of the Apocalypse, which contains a doctrine absolutely identical with that which the Church teaches on the same matter. For the same reason, therefore, no chapter of Scripture has the same sense for the critic and the theologian.

62. The chief articles of the Apostles' Creed did not have the same sense for the Christians of the first ages as they have for the Christians of our time.

63. The Church shows that she is incapable of effectively maintaining evangelical ethics since she obstinately clings to immutable doctrines which cannot be reconciled with modern progress.

64. Scientific progress demands that the concepts of Christian doctrine concerning God, creation, revelation, the Person of the incarnate Word, and Redemption be readjusted.

65. Modern Catholicism can be reconciled with true science only if it is transformed into a non-dogmatic Christianity; that is to say, into a broad and liberal Protestantism.

The following Thursday, the fourth day of the same month and year, all these matters were accurately reported to our Most Holy Lord, Pope Pius X. His Holiness approved and confirmed the decree of the Most Eminent Fathers and ordered that each and every one of the above-listed propositions be held by all as condemned and proscribed.

Sacrorum Antistitum

MOTU PROPRIO ESTABLISHING THE OATH AGAINST MODERNISM *AND CERTAIN LAWS FOR THE DRIVING OUT OF THE DANGER OF MODERNISM*

Pope Pius X

September 1, 1910

Danger of Modernism

1. None of the bishops, we believe, can have failed to observe how that most cunning class of persons, the Modernists, though unmasked by the Encyclical Letter *Pascendi Dominici Gregis*,[122] have not abandoned their designs on the peace of the Church. For they continue to enroll new associates and to band them together in a secret alliance, and with these they are now engaged in inoculating into the veins of the Christian people the poison of their opinions by means of books and pamphlets published anonymously or under false names. To those who read again and more closely the document just mentioned, it will be clear that this climax of audacity, which has caused us such grief, proves that these men are really as we described them, and enemies all the more to be feared by reason of their proximity, and who abuse their ministry to catch by their poisoned bait those who are not on their guard and who are liable to be led astray by a semblance of science which contains the germs of all errors.

Pastoral Duty

2. But as this pest is spreading in a part of the field of the Lord from which the fairest fruits were to be expected, if it is the duty of all the

[122] September 8, 1907.

pastors to labor for the defense of the Catholic Faith, and to use the utmost vigilance that the divine deposit suffer no hurt, upon us especially rests the charge of realizing the commands of Christ the Savior, Who said to Peter, whose supreme authority we, unworthy though we are, have received: "Confirm thy brethren" (Lk 22:32). And this is why we deem it well in the present conflict to recall to memory the following teachings and rulings contained in our letter abovementioned:[123]

> We beg and conjure you to see to it that in this most grave matter nobody will ever be able to say that you have been in the slightest degree wanting in vigilance or zeal or firmness. And what we ask of you and expect of you we ask and expect also of all other pastors of souls, of all educators and professors of clerics, and in a very special way of the superiors of religious institutions.
>
> In the first place, with regard to studies, we will and ordain that scholastic philosophy be made the basis of the sacred sciences. It goes without saying that "if anything is met with among the scholastic doctors which may be regarded as an excess of subtlety, or which does not square with later discoveries, or which is altogether destitute of probability, we have no desire whatever to propose it for the imitation of present generations."[124] And let it be clearly understood above all things that the scholastic philosophy we prescribe is that which the Angelic Doctor has bequeathed to us, and we, therefore, declare that all the ordinances of Our predecessor on this subject continue fully in force, and, as far as may be necessary, we do decree anew, and confirm, and ordain that they be by all strictly observed. In seminaries where they may have been neglected, let the bishops impose them and require their observance, and let this apply also to the superiors of religious institutions. Further, let professors remember that they cannot set St. Thomas aside, especially in metaphysical questions, without grave detriment. "A small error at the beginning," to use the words of Aquinas, "becomes great in the end."[125]

[123] *Pascendi Dominici Gregis*, nos. 44–56.

[124] Pope Leo XIII, Encyclical *Aeterni Patris* (August 4, 1879), no. 31.

[125] *De Ente et Essentia*, proëm.

On this philosophical foundation the theological edifice is to be solidly raised. Promote the study of theology, Venerable Brothers, by all means in your power, so that your clerics on leaving the seminaries may admire and love it and always find their delight in it. "For in the vast and varied abundance of studies opening before the mind desirous of truth, everybody knows how the old maxim describes theology as so far in front of all others that every science and art should serve it and be to it as handmaidens."[126] We will add that we deem as worthy of praise those who with full respect for Tradition, the holy Fathers, the ecclesiastical Magisterium, undertake, with well-balanced judgment and guided by Catholic principles (which is not always the case), seek to illuminate positive theology by throwing the light of true history upon it. Certainly, more attention must be paid to positive theology than in the past, but this must be done without detriment to scholastic theology, and those are to be disapproved as of Modernist tendencies who exalt positive theology in such a way as to seem to despise the scholastic.

With regard to profane studies, suffice it to recall here what Our predecessor has admirably said: "Apply yourselves energetically to the study of natural sciences: the brilliant discoveries and the bold and useful applications of them made in our times, which have won such applause from our contemporaries, will be an object of perpetual praise for those that come after us."[127] But do this without interfering with sacred studies, as Our predecessor urges in these most grave words: "If you carefully search for the cause of these errors you will find that it lies in the fact that these days, when the natural sciences absorb so much study, the more severe and lofty studies have been proportionately neglected—some of them have almost passed into oblivion, some of them are pursued in a half-hearted or superficial way, and, sad to say, now that they are fallen from their old estate, they have been disfigured by perverse doctrines and monstrous errors."[128] We ordain therefore that the study of natural science in the seminaries be carried on under this law.

[126] Pope Leo XIII, Apostolic Letter (December 10, 1889), *In magna*.
[127] Pope Leo XIII, Allocution *Pergratus Nobis* (March 7, 1880).
[128] Pope Leo XIII, *Pergratus Nobis*.

All these prescriptions and those of Our predecessor are to be borne in mind whenever there is question of choosing directors and professors for seminaries and Catholic universities. Anybody who in any way is found to be imbued with Modernism is to be excluded without compunction from these offices, and those who already occupy them are to be removed. The same policy is to be adopted toward those who favor Modernism either by extolling the Modernists or excusing their culpable conduct, or by criticizing scholasticism and the holy Fathers, or by refusing obedience to ecclesiastical authority in any of its depositaries; and toward those who show a love of novelty in history, archeology, biblical exegesis, and finally toward those who neglect the sacred sciences or appear to prefer to them the profane. In all this question of studies, Venerable Brothers, you cannot be too watchful or too constant, but most of all in the choice of professors, for as a rule the students are modeled after the pattern of their masters. Strong in the consciousness of your duty, act always prudently but vigorously.

Equal diligence and severity are to be used in examining and selecting candidates for holy orders. Far, far from the clergy be the love of novelty! God hates the proud and the obstinate. For the future, the doctorate of theology and canon law must never be conferred on anybody who has not made the regular course of scholastic philosophy; if conferred, it shall be held as null and void. The rules laid down in 1896 by the Sacred Congregation of Bishops and Regulars for the clerics, both secular and regular, of Italy concerning the frequenting of the universities we now decree to be extended to all nations.[129] Clerics and priests inscribed in a Catholic institute or university must not in the future follow in civil universities those courses for which there are chairs in the Catholic institutes to which they belong. If this have been permitted anywhere in the past, we ordain that it be not allowed for the future. Let the bishops who form the governing board of such Catholic institutes or universities watch with all care that these our commands be constantly observed.

[129] July 21, 1896, in *Acta Sanctae Sedis* [ASS], 29:359–364.

It is also the duty of the bishops to prevent writings infected with Modernism or favorable to it from being read when they have been published, and to hinder their publication when they have not. No book or paper or periodical of this kind must ever be permitted to seminarists or university students. The injury to them would be equal to that caused by immoral reading; nay, it would be greater, for such writings poison Christian life at its very fount. The same decision is to be taken concerning the writings of some Catholics, who, though not badly disposed themselves, but ill-instructed in theological studies and imbued with modern philosophy, strive to make this harmonize with the Faith, and, as they say, to turn it to the account of the Faith. The name and reputation of these authors causes them to be read without suspicion, and they are therefore all the more dangerous in preparing the way for Modernism.

To give you some more general directions, Venerable Brothers, in a matter of such moment, we bid you do everything in your power to drive out of your dioceses, even by solemn interdict, any pernicious books that may be in circulation there. The Holy See neglects no means to put down writings of this kind, but the number of them has now grown to such an extent that it is impossible to censure them all. Hence it happens that the medicine sometimes arrives too late, for the disease has taken root during the delay. We will, therefore, that the bishops, putting aside all fear and the prudence of the flesh, despising the outcries of the wicked, gently by all means, but constantly, do each his own share of this work, remembering the injunctions of Leo XIII in the Apostolic Constitution *Officiorum*: "Let the ordinaries, acting in this also as delegates of the Apostolic See, exert themselves to proscribe and to put out of reach of the faithful injurious books or other writings printed or circulated in their dioceses."[130] In this passage, the bishops, it is true, receive a right, but they have also a duty imposed on them. Let no bishop think that he fulfills this duty by denouncing to us one or two books, while a great many others of the same kind are being published and circulated. Nor are you to be deterred by the fact

[130] *Officiorum ac munerum* (January 25, 1897), tit. 1, chap. 10, art. 27.

that a book has obtained the *Imprimatur* elsewhere, both because this may be merely simulated and because it may have been granted through carelessness, or easiness, or excessive confidence in the author, as may sometimes happen in religious orders. Besides, just as the same food does not agree equally with everybody, it may happen that a book, harmless in one place, may on account of the different circumstances be hurtful in another. Should a bishop, therefore, after having taken the advice of prudent persons, deem it right to condemn any of such books in his diocese, we not only give him ample faculty to do so, but we impose it upon him as a duty to do so. Of course, it is our wish that in such cases the proper regards be used, and sometimes it will suffice to restrict the prohibition to the clergy; but, even in such cases, it will be obligatory on Catholic booksellers not to put on sale the books condemned by the bishop.

And while we are on this subject of booksellers, we wish the bishops to see to it that they do not, through desire for gain, put on sale unsound books. It is certain that in the catalogues of some of them the books of the Modernists are not unfrequently announced with no small praise. If they refuse obedience, let the bishops have no hesitation in depriving them of the title of Catholic booksellers; so, too, and with more reason, if they have the title of Episcopal booksellers, and if they have that of Pontifical, let them be denounced to the Apostolic See. Finally, we remind all of the twenty-sixth article of the abovementioned Constitution *Officiorum*: "All those who have obtained an apostolic faculty to read and keep forbidden books are not thereby authorized to read books and periodicals forbidden by the local ordinaries, unless the apostolic faculty expressly concedes permission to read and keep books condemned by anybody."

But it is not enough to hinder the reading and the sale of bad books—it is also necessary to prevent them from being printed. Hence let the bishops use the utmost severity in granting permission to print. Under the rules of the Constitution *Officiorum*, a great many publications require the authorization of the ordinary, and in some dioceses it has been made the custom to have a suitable number of official censors for the examination of writings. We have the highest praise for this institution, and we not only exhort, but we order that it be extended to all dioceses. In all episcopal curias, therefore, let censors be appointed for the revision of works intended for publication, and let the censors, to be chosen from both ranks of the clergy, be men of age, knowledge, and prudence, who will know how to follow the golden mean in their judgments. It shall be their office to examine everything which requires permission for publication according to Articles 41 and 42 of the abovementioned constitution. The censor shall give his verdict in writing. If it be favorable, the bishop will give the permission for publication by the word *Imprimatur*, which must always be preceded by the *Nihil obstat* and the name of the censor. In the Curia of Rome official censors shall be appointed just as elsewhere, and the appointment of them shall appertain to the Master of the Sacred Palaces, after they have been proposed to the Cardinal Vicar and accepted by the Sovereign Pontiff. It shall also be the office of the Master of the Sacred Palaces to select the censor for each writing. Permission for publication shall be granted by him as well as by the Cardinal Vicar or his vicegerent, and this permission, as above prescribed, must always be preceded by the *Nihil obstat* and the name of the censor. Only on very rare and exceptional occasions, and on the prudent decision of the bishop, shall it be permissible to omit mention of the censor. The name of the censor shall never be made known to the authors until he have given a favorable decision, so that he may not have to suffer annoyance either while he is engaged in the examination of a writing or in case he should deny his approval. Censors shall never be chosen from the religious orders until the opinion of the provincial, or in Rome of the general, have been privately obtained, and the provincial or the general must give a conscientious account of the character, knowledge, and orthodoxy of the candidate. We admonish religious superiors of their solemn duty never to allow anything to be published by any of their subjects without permission from themselves and from the ordinary. Finally, we affirm and declare that the title of censor has no value and can never be adduced to give credit to the private opinions of the person who holds it.

Having said this much in general, we now ordain in particular a more careful observance of Article 42 of the abovementioned Constitution *Officiorum*. It is "forbidden to secular priests, without the previous consent of the ordinary, to undertake the direction of papers or periodicals." This permission shall be withdrawn from any priest who makes a wrong use of it, after having been admonished. With regard to priests who are "correspondents" or "collaborators" of periodicals, as it happens not unfrequently that they write matter infected with Modernism for their papers or periodicals, let the bishops see to it that this is not permitted to happen, and should it happen, let them warn the writers or prevent them from writing. The superiors of religious orders, too, we admonish with all authority to do the same, and should they fail in this duty, let the bishops make due provision with authority delegated by the Supreme Pontiff. Let there be, as far as this is possible, a special censor for newspapers and periodicals printed by Catholics. It shall be his office to read in due time each number after it has been published, and if he find anything dangerous in it, let him order that it be corrected. The bishop shall have the same right even when the censor has seen nothing objectionable in a publication.

We have already mentioned congresses and public gatherings as among the means used by the Modernists to defend and propagate their opinions. In the future, bishops shall not permit congresses of priests except on very rare occasions. When they do permit them, it shall only be on condition that matters appertaining to the bishop or the Apostolic See be not treated in them, and that no motions or postulates be allowed that would imply a usurpation of sacred authority, and that no mention be made in them of Modernism, Presbyterianism, or laicism. At congresses of this kind, which can only be held after permission in writing has been obtained in due time and for each case, it shall not be lawful for priests from other dioceses to take part without the written permission of their ordinary. Further, no priest must lose sight of the solemn recommendation of Leo XIII: "Let priests hold as sacred the authority of their pastors, let them take it for certain that the sacerdotal ministry, if not exercised under the guidance of the bishops, can never be either holy, or very fruitful, or respectable."[131]

But of what avail, Venerable Brothers, will be all Our commands and prescriptions, if they be not dutifully and firmly carried out? And in order that this may be done, it has seemed expedient to Us to extend to all dioceses the regulations laid down with great wisdom many years ago by the bishops of Umbria for theirs: "In order," they say, "to extirpate the errors already propagated and to prevent their further diffusion and to remove those teachers of impiety through whom the pernicious effects of such diffusion are being perpetuated, this sacred assembly, following the example of St. Charles Borromeo, has decided to establish in each of the dioceses a council consisting of approved members of both branches of the clergy, which shall be charged with the task of noting the existence of errors and the devices by which new ones are introduced and propagated, and to inform the bishop of the whole, so that he may take counsel with them as to the best means for nipping the evil in the bud and preventing it spreading for the ruin of souls, or, worse still, gaining strength and growth."[132] We decree therefore that in every diocese a council of this kind, which We are pleased to name "The Council of Vigilance," be instituted without delay. The priests called to form part of it shall be chosen somewhat after the manner above prescribed for the censors, and they shall meet every two months on an appointed day under the presidency of the bishop. They shall be bound to secrecy as to their deliberations and decisions, and their function shall be as follows: They shall watch most carefully for every trace and sign of Modernism, both in publications and in teaching, and, to preserve from it the clergy and the young, they shall take all prudent, prompt, and efficacious measures. Let them combat novelties of words, remembering the admonitions of Leo XIII: "It is impossible to approve in Catholic publications of a style inspired by unsound novelty which seems to deride the piety of the faithful and dwells on the introduction of a new order of Christian life, on new directions of the Church,

[131] Encyclical *Nobilissima Gallorum* (February 8, 1884), no. 8.
[132] Acts of the Congress of Bishops of Umbria (November, 1849), tit. 2, art. 6.

on new aspirations of the modern soul, on a new vocation of the clergy, on a new Christian civilization."[133] Language of this kind is not to be tolerated either in books or from chairs of learning. The councils must not neglect the books treating of the pious traditions of different places or of sacred relics. Let them not permit such questions to be discussed in periodicals destined to stimulate piety, neither with expressions that savor of mockery or contempt, nor by dogmatic pronouncements, especially when, as is often the case, what is stated as a certainty either does not pass the limits of probability or is merely based on prejudiced opinions. Concerning sacred relics, let this be the rule: When the bishops, who alone are judges in these matters, know for certain that a relic is not genuine, let them remove it at once from the veneration of the faithful; if the authentications of a relic happen to have been lost through political disturbances or in some other way, let it not be exposed for public veneration until the bishop has verified it. The argument of prescription or well-founded presumption is to have weight only when devotion to a relic is commendable by reason of its antiquity, according to the sense of the decree issued in 1896 by the Congregation of Indulgences and Sacred Relics: "Ancient relics are to enjoy the veneration they have always enjoyed except in those individual instances when there are clear arguments that they are false or supposititious." In passing judgment on pious traditions be it always be borne in mind that in this matter the Church uses such prudence that she does not permit traditions of this kind to be narrated in books except with the utmost caution and with the insertion of the declaration imposed by Urban VIII; and even then she does not guarantee the truth of the fact narrated: she simply does not forbid belief in things for which human arguments are not wanting. On this matter the Sacred Congregation of Rites thirty years ago decreed as follows: "These apparitions have neither been approved nor condemned by the Holy See, which has simply allowed that they be believed on purely human faith, on the traditions that relate them, corroborated by testimonies and documents

[133] Instruction of the Sacred Congregation of Extraordinary Ecclesiastical Affairs (January 27, 1902), in ASS, 34:409.

'worthy of credence.'"[134] Anybody who follows this rule has no cause for fear. For the devotion based on any apparition, in as far as it regards the fact itself, that is to say, in as far as it is "relative," always implies the hypothesis of the truth of the fact; while in as far as it is "absolute," it must always be based on the truth, seeing that its object is the persons of the saints who are honored. The same is true of relics. Finally, we entrust to the Councils of Vigilance the duty of overlooking assiduously and diligently social institutions as well as writings on social questions, so that they may harbor no trace of Modernism, but obey the prescriptions of the Roman Pontiffs.

Lest what we have laid down thus far should fall into oblivion, we will and ordain that the bishops of all dioceses a year after this publication and every three years thenceforward furnish the Holy See with a diligent and sworn report on all the prescriptions contained in them, and on the doctrines that find currency among the clergy, and especially in the seminaries and other Catholic institutions, and we impose the like obligation on the generals of religious orders with regard to those under them.

Seminary and Religious Studies

3. To all this, which we fully confirm under pain of temerarious conscience upon those who refuse to hearken to our words, we now add some special instruction concerning ecclesiastical students in the seminaries and aspirants in religious institutes. In the seminaries all the parts of the institutions must be directed to the formation of priests worthy of the name. For it must not be thought that such institutions are destined merely for study or for piety—they combine both these; they are the training schools in which the army of Christ is built up by a long course of preparation. In order that a host thoroughly equipped may come forth from them, two things are fundamentally necessary: doctrine for the culture of the mind, virtue for the perfection of the soul. The

[134] Decree (December 11, 1878), in ASS, 11:513, rep. 2.

former of these demands that ecclesiastical students be highly enlightened in those branches which are closely connected with the studies of divine things; the latter demands a special degree of virtue and constancy. Let the superiors of discipline and piety, therefore, note what promise the individual students give of themselves and study their characters—whether they give themselves up unduly to their natural bent, whether they show worldly tendencies; whether they are docile to obey, given to piety, not having an exalted idea of themselves, observant of discipline; whether they are led to aspire to the priesthood by a right aim or by human motives; whether their lives are marked by the holiness and doctrine suitable to their state, or at least, if there be any defect in this respect, do they endeavor sincerely and willingly to acquire it. Nor does this investigation present excessive difficulties; for the lack of virtue referred to is speedily produced by a hypocritical performance of the offices of religion and by the observance of discipline through fear rather than at the dictates of conscience, and the person who observes discipline through servile fear, or violates it through levity of mind or through contempt, is very far from offering a guarantee of living worthily in the priesthood. For it is not easy to believe that he who despises domestic discipline will not fall away from the public laws of the Church. When a superior of sacred youth finds one of them in this frame of mind and, after warning him once or twice, notes no change for the better after a year of trial, he should expel him in such a way as to render it impossible for such a student to be again received either by himself or by any bishop.

4. Two things, therefore, are primarily necessary in promoting clerics: innocence of life joined with soundness of doctrine. Nor must it be forgotten that the precepts and admonitions addressed by the bishops to those whom they are initiating in sacred orders are meant as much for themselves as for the candidates; as, for instance, when it is laid down: "Care must be taken that heavenly

wisdom, upright life, and long observance of justice commend the elect for this office.... Let them be upright and ripe at once in knowledge and in works;... let the form of all justice shine forth in them."

5. With regard to probity of life it would not be necessary to say more were it possible to separate this easily from the doctrines and opinions which a man takes it upon him to defend. But, as we read in the book of Proverbs: "A man shall be known by his doctrine" (12:8), and as the apostle teaches: "Whosoever continueth not in the doctrine of Christ hath not God" (2 Jn 1:9). How much of effort is to be spent in acquiring knowledge of many and various things may be seen from the very conditions of the age which proclaims that the light of progressing humanity is the most glorious of achievements. All the clergy, therefore, who wish to perform their duties in a manner worthy of the time, fruitfully "to exhort in sound doctrine and to convince the gainsayers" (Ti 1:9), to devote the resources of intellect to the utility of the Church, must acquire a knowledge of things beyond the common and approach as closely as possible to the perfection of doctrine. For the fight is one with enemies not lacking in skill, whose polished studies are not unfrequently united with a science full of wiles and whose specious and vibrant sentences are made up of impetuous and sounding phrases, so as to make it appear that they contain something entirely new. Hence we must carefully prepare our arms, that is, a rich fund of doctrine is to be acquired by all those who are preparing themselves in retirement for the holiest and most arduous of tasks.

6. But since the life of man is circumscribed within such limits that it is barely possible for one to learn cursorily something of the immense fund of things that are to be known, the thirst for knowledge must be regulated and the sentence of Paul be acted upon: "Not to be more wise than it behooveth to be wise, but to be wise unto sobriety" (Rom 12:3). Hence as clerics are already sufficiently burdened

with the many important studies imposed upon them relating to sacred literature, to the points of faith, morals, the science of piety, and offices known as ascetics, to the history of the Church, canon law, and sacred eloquence, in order that the students may not waste their time in the pursuit of other questions and be distracted from the main objects of their studies, we absolutely forbid that any journals or periodicals, however excellent, be read by them, binding the consciences of the superiors to take care scrupulously that this does not happen.

Vigilance against Modernism

7. To remove all suspicion of the secret introduction of Modernism, we not only will the absolute observance of the prescriptions contained in No. 2 above, but we ordain, moreover, that the individual professors before inaugurating their lectures at the beginning of the year shall present to the bishop the text they propose to use in teaching or the questions or theses which are to be treated; then that the teaching of each of them be examined during the year, and should it appear that this is not in harmony with sound doctrine, the fact shall be held sufficient to have the professor removed there and then. Finally, in addition to the profession of faith, each professor shall take an oath according to the formula given below before his bishop and shall sign his name to it.

8. This oath, after the profession of faith, in the form prescribed by Our predecessor, Pius IV, of holy memory, has been made, together with accompanying definitions of the Vatican Council, shall be taken in presence of the bishop by:

> I. Clerics who are to be initiated in major orders: to each of whom a copy shall be previously presented both of the profession of faith and of the form of oath, so that they may know accurately what they are, and with them the penalties incurred by violation of the oath.

II. Priests appointed for hearing confessions and sacred preachers, before they receive faculties for exercising these sacred offices.

III. Parish priests, canons, holders of livings, before they enter on possession of their benefices.

IV. Officials in the episcopal curias and ecclesiastical tribunals, not excepting the vicar general and the judges.

V. Lenten preachers.

VI. All officials in the Roman Congregations or Tribunals before the Cardinal Prefect or Cardinal Secretary of the same.

VII. The superiors and professors of religious families and congregations, before they enter on office.

9. The formula of the profession of faith, mentioned above, and of the oath are to be kept in special frames in all episcopal curias as well as in the different offices of the Roman Congregations. And should anybody dare, which may God forbid, to violate the oath, he is to be delated at once to the Holy Office.

OATH FORMULA

I ... firmly hold and accept each and every definition of the unerring teaching of the Church, with all she has maintained and declared, but especially those points of doctrine which expressly combat the errors of our time.

In the first place, I profess my belief that God, the beginning and end of all, can be surely known and also proved to exist by the natural light of reason from the things that are made, that is, from the visible works of the creation as a cause from its effects.

Next, I recognize and acknowledge the external arguments of revelation, that is, divine facts, especially miracles and prophecies, as the surest signs of the divine origin of the Christian religion, and

I hold that these are specially suited to the understanding of every age and of all men, even of our times.

Thirdly, I likewise hold with firm faith that the Church, the guardian and exponent of the revealed Word, was proximately and directly founded by Christ Himself, the true Person of history, while He dwelt amongst us, and that she was also built upon Peter, the Prince of the Apostolic Hierarchy, and upon his successors to the end of time.

Fourthly, I sincerely receive the teaching of faith as transmitted in the same sense and meaning right down to us; and, therefore, I wholly reject the heretical notion of the evolution of dogmas, which pass from one sense to another alien to that the Church held from the start; and I likewise condemn every error whereby is substituted for the divine deposit, entrusted by Christ to His Spouse and by her to be faithfully guarded, a philosophic system or a creation of the human conscience, gradually refined by the striving of men and finally to be perfected hereafter by indefinite progress.

Fifthly, I hold for certain and sincerely profess that faith is not a blind religious sense making its way out of the hidden regions of the subliminal consciousness, morally tinged by the influence of heart and will, but is a true assent of the intellect to truth received from without by hearing, an assent whereby we believe to be true, because of the authority of the all-true God, whatever by the personal God, our Creator and Lord, has been spoken, testified, and revealed.

I further, with all due reverence, submit and with my whole mind adhere to all the condemnations, declarations, and directions contained in the Encyclical Letter *Pascendi* and in the Decree *Lamentabili*, particularly regarding what is called the history of dogma.

I also reject the error of those who allege that the Faith proposed by the Church may be in conflict with history and that Catholic dogmas in the sense in which they are now understood cannot be harmonized with the more truthful "origins" of Christianity.

Moreover, I condemn and reject the opinion which declares that a Christian man of better culture can assume a dual personality, one as believer and another as historian, thus taking it to be permissible for the historian to hold fast what his faith as a believer contradicts, or to lay down premises from which there follows the falsity or the uncertainty of dogmas, provided only that these are not directly denied.

Likewise, I reject that method of estimating and interpreting Holy Writ which, setting aside the Church's Tradition and the analogy of faith and the rules of the Apostolic See, adopts the rationalists' principles and with equal arbitrariness and rashness considers criticism of the text the one only supreme rule.

In like manner, I reprobate the opinion of those who hold that a teacher of the science of historical theology or the writer on the subject must first put aside the notions previously conceived about the supernatural origin of Catholic Tradition or about the divine aid promised for the perpetual preservation of each revealed truth; then that the writings of individual Fathers must be interpreted solely by the data of science, without any reference to sacred authority, and with the freedom of judgment wherewith every profane record is usually examined.

Finally and in general, I declare myself to be far removed from the error of the Modernists who hold that in Sacred Tradition there is nothing inherently divine; or who—far worse still—admit it in a pantheistic sense: thus there would remain only a bare simple fact equal to the ordinary facts of history, viz., that the school started by Christ and His apostles still finds men to support it by their energy, their shrewdness, their ability.

Wherefore most firmly I retain and to my last breath will I retain the Faith of the Fathers of the Church concerning the sure endowment of truth, which is, has been, and ever will be in the succession of the episcopate from the apostles;[135] not in such a way that we may hold what seems best and most fitting according to the refinement of each age, but that we never in any different wise understand the

[135] See St. Irenaeus, *Adversus haereses*, bk. 4, chap. 26.

absolute and unchangeable truth preached from the beginning by the apostles.[136]

All this I promise that I will faithfully, entirely, and sincerely keep and inviolably guard, and from this never in teaching or howsoever by word or writing in the least depart. So I promise, so I swear, so help me God, etc.

On Sacred Preaching

10. Since long experience has taught us that the zeal of the bishops in providing for the preaching of the divine Word has not produced its proper fruit, not, we think, on account of the negligence of the hearers, but on account of the vanity of preachers whose words are the words of men rather than of God, we deem it well to reproduce here in Latin and to recommend to the ordinaries the document[137] issued at the command of Our predecessor, Leo XIII, of happy memory, by the Sacred Congregation of Bishops and Regulars on July 31, 1894, and sent to the ordinaries of Italy and to the superiors of religious families and congregations:

> And in the first place as regards the ornament of virtue, which should above all distinguish sacred orators, let the ordinaries and the superiors of religious families take good care never to entrust this holy and salutary mission of the divine Word to those whose piety toward God and love of His Son Christ Our Lord does not shine forth. For if the preachers of Catholic doctrine be lacking in these qualities, they will never be anything but "a sounding brass and a tinkling cymbal" (1 Cor 13:1), and they will always be destitute of that which forms the whole strength and efficacy of evangelical preaching, that is, zeal for the glory of God and the salvation of souls. And this piety, so necessary for sacred orators, must shine forth even in their external conduct in order that their lives may not be in opposition with the Christian precepts and institutions

[136] See Tertullian, *De praescriptione haereticorum*, chap. 28.
[137] See ASS, 27:162–176.

which they extol in their discourses and that they may not destroy by their acts what they build up by their words. Again, there must be nothing profane in this piety, but rather let it be instinct with that gravity which reveals them as "the ministers of Christ and the dispensers of the divine mysteries" (1 Cor 4:1). For otherwise, as the Angelic Doctor well says, "if the doctrine is good and the preacher bad, the latter is an occasion of blasphemy against the doctrine of God."[138] But piety and the other Christian virtues must have knowledge as their inseparable companion, since it is obvious and clearly proved by long experience that the Word cannot be suitably and fruitfully preached by men destitute of knowledge, especially sacred knowledge, who, trusting to a certain natural facility in elocution, boldly ascend the pulpit without any preparation. Such as they beat the air, and all unconsciously expose divine revelation to derision and contempt and put themselves on a level with those of whom the divine words were spoken: "Because thou hast rejected knowledge, I will reject thee, that thou shalt not do the office of priesthood to Me" (Os 4:6).

Therefore bishops and superiors of religious communities must not entrust the ministry of the divine Word to any priest who has not proved himself to be sufficiently endowed with piety and knowledge. They are to take great care, too, that only subjects worthy of sacred eloquence be treated in the pulpit. These have been indicated by Our Lord when He said: "Preach the gospel" (Mk 16:15). "Teaching them to observe all things whatsoever I have commanded you" (Mt 28:20), words which are thus suitably explained by St. Thomas: "Preachers must enlighten in faith, direct in works, point out what is to be avoided, and, by threats and promises, lead men to truth and goodness."[139] And the Council of Trent adds: "Let them preach the extirpation of vice and the practice of virtue to avoid eternal punishment and gain the glory of heaven,"[140] in development of which Pius IX, of happy memory, has written: "They must preach not themselves, but Christ Crucified; let them,

[138] *Comm. in Matthaeum* (*Corpus Thomisticum Petri de Scala*), chap. 5, lect. 5.
[139] *Comm. in Matthaeum* (*Corpus Thomisticum Petri de Scala*), chap. 5, lect. 4.
[140] Session V, *Decree on Reformation*, chap. 2.

then, announce to the people, clearly and simply, with grave and persuasive eloquence and according to the doctrine of the Catholic Church and of the Fathers, the dogmas and precepts of our most holy religion; let them carefully explain to the people the special duties of each, turn them from vice and kindle them in charity, so that the faithful, healthily strengthened by the Word of God, may abandon vice, practice virtue, and thus be enabled to avoid eternal punishment and win the glory of heaven."[141] From all this it will be clear that the proper subjects for preaching are the Apostles' Creed, the Ten Commandments, the precepts of the Church, the sacraments, the virtues and vices, the duties of one's state of life, the four last things, and other eternal truths of the same kind.

But today the ministers of the divine Word only too often pay but small attention to this rich and important mine of subjects; they neglect it and almost reject it as something useless and superannuated. Knowing well as they do that the topics we have just enumerated are little calculated to win popular applause, for which they are so eager, and "seeking their own interests and not those of Jesus Christ" (Phil 2:21), they thrust aside these topics even during Lent and the most solemn seasons of the year. And changing names as well as things, they substitute for the old instructions a new and not very intelligible kind of discourse, which they call "conferences," far better adapted to flatter intellect and thought than to control the will and reform conduct. They do not reflect that while moral instructions are useful for all, conferences are so only to a few, and that even these few, if the orator occupied himself more with their conduct by frequently inculcating chastity, humility of heart, obedience to the authority of the Church, would thus be freed from their prejudices against the Faith and receive the light of truth with better dispositions. For if there are many, especially in Catholic countries, who have false ideas regarding religion, the fact is to be attributed to the unchecked passions of the heart rather than to aberration of the mind, according to the divine sentence: "From the heart come forth evil thoughts,... blasphemies" (Mt 15:19). Thus

[141] *Qui Pluribus*, no. 26.

St. Augustine, referring to the words of the psalmist, "the fool hath said in his heart: There is no God" (Ps 13:1), says: "It is the heart, not the mind, that speaks here."

This does not imply, however, that discourses of this kind are to be absolutely condemned, for when they are well done they may often prove very useful and even necessary to refute errors contrary to religion. But it is necessary to banish absolutely from the pulpit that elaborate style of address which concerns theory more than practice, which concerns the civil more closely than the religious order, and which is more notable for its external show than for the fruit that follows from it. All that elaboration which is better suited for meetings or learned gatherings is quite out of touch with the majesty of the house of God. As regards lectures or conferences which aim at the defense of religion against attack, very necessary as they are in certain cases, they are not within the capacity of all, but only of the best equipped; and even the best speakers should not hold these conferences except when time and place and the condition of the hearers render them necessary and there is some hope of their doing good—and this, it will be clear to all, is a point which must be left to the legitimate verdict of the ordinary. In these discourses, too, the power of conviction should be based rather on sacred doctrine than on the words of human wisdom, and that the exposition should be made with force and clearness, so that error may not make a deeper impression than truth on the minds of the hearers, and objections be not stronger than the answers given to them. But above all things, care must be taken that the frequency of such discourses shall not diminish that of moral instructions, and that the importance of the latter be not minimized as though, being of an inferior order, they were less worthy of respect than the others and were therefore to be left to ordinary preachers and hearers; for the truth is, on the contrary, that moral instructions are absolutely necessary for the majority of the faithful and are not less in dignity than apologetic dissertations, so that even the best orators, at least from time to time and before the best classes of hearers, should devote themselves with the greatest care to this kind of sermons. If a contrary practice is followed, the faithful are forever being obliged to listen to discourses about errors from which the majority of them are immune and never of the faults and vices they really possess.

But if there is reason to complain about the choice of subjects, there are other reasons and grave ones as regards the style and form of the sermons preached. St. Thomas well teaches that to be really "the light of the world, the preacher of the divine Word must possess three things: first, solidity, so that he may not fall away from the truth; second, clearness, so that he may not teach it obscurely; third, a useful aim, so that he may seek God's glory and not his own."[142] Too often the style of contemporary eloquence is not only at variance with the clearness of that evangelical simplicity which it should possess, but is mostly made up of clashing words and recondite thoughts beyond the grasp of the people. This is deplorable and to be lamented in the words of the prophet: "The little ones asked for bread and there was no one to break it for them" (Lam 4:4). But even more lamentable still is the fact that so many sermons are destitute of the religious spirit, the atmosphere of Christian piety, that divine force and virtue of the Holy Spirit which appeals to the soul and leads it gently to what is right—a force and virtue which should always assimilate preaching to the words of the apostle: "My speech and my preaching was not in the persuasive words of human wisdom, but in showing of the Spirit and power" (1 Cor 2:4). But those who place their reliance in the persuasive words of human wisdom rarely if ever have recourse to the divine sources and to the Sacred Scriptures, that contain those living waters which are the most fruitful and abundant matter for sacred preaching, as [His Holiness Leo XIII] eloquently explained recently in these grave words:

> Herein is to be found the proper and special virtues of the Scriptures, from the divine breath of the Holy Spirit, Who confers authority on the preacher, endows him with apostolic liberty of speech, and inspires him with forceful and triumphant eloquence. Such a speaker reproduces the spirit and force of the divine Word, his preaching "is not in word

[142] *Comm. in Matthaeum* (*Corpus Thomisticum Petri de Scala*), chap. 5, lect. 4.

> only, but in power also, and in the Holy Ghost and in much fullness" (1 Thes 1:5). Hence it must be said that inconsistent and thoughtless is the conduct of those who deliver addresses on religion and announce the divine commandments in the mere words of human science and prudence instead of availing themselves of the only means that are divine. Their language, empty of the fire of the Word of God, necessarily languishes and grows cold and possesses nothing of that divine virtue which shines forth in the divine Word. "The Word of God is living and effectual and more piercing than any two-edged sword, and reaching unto the division of the soul and the spirit" (Heb 4:12). Thinking men must recognize that there is in the Sacred Writings an eloquence truly wonderful and varied and worthy of the great things it expresses. Augustine understood this and expatiated on it with skill;[143] and experience shows that the greatest sacred orators, and they have recognized it themselves, owe their reputation to their assiduous use and pious meditation of the Bible.[144]

The Bible is, therefore, the chief source of sacred eloquence. But preachers eager after new models instead of going to the "living source," turn deplorably to "the broken cisterns of human wisdom" (see Jer 2:13), and, neglecting the divinely inspired doctrine of the Fathers of the Church and the councils, lose themselves entirely in quoting the names and phrases of modern and still living profane writers—phrases which very often give rise to very dangerous interpretations or misunderstandings.

> They offend again by speaking of religion as if they wished to measure everything according to the standard of the goods and advantages of this ephemeral life, with hardly any reference to a future and eternal life; by dilating on the fruits which the Christian religion has brought to human

[143] See *De Doctrina Christiana*, bk. 4, chaps. 6–7.
[144] Encyclical *Providentissimus Deus* (November 18, 1893), no. 4.

> society, but omitting to dwell on the duties which it imposes; by exalting the charity of Christ the Savior, but without speaking of His justice. Hence the small fruit derived from such preaching, from which the profane hearer rises with the impression that he can, without changing his conduct, be a Christian merely by saying: "I believe in Jesus Christ."[145]

But what care they for the fruits of their preaching—it is not of these they are thinking. Their one great care is to flatter their hearers by tickling their ears (see 2 Tm 4:3). It is enough for them that the churches are full, even if the hearts of the people in them are empty. Hence they never make any mention of the remission of sins, of the four last things, and of other capital questions; they speak only to please, and they think only of extracting cries of admiration and applause by a profane eloquence better fitted for speechmakers than for those engaged in the apostolic and sacred ministry. Against such as these St. Jerome writes: "When you teach in the church, let the people utter not exclamations, but groans; let the tears of your hearers be your praise."[146] Hence it happens that these instructions, both within and without the precincts of the church, take on a theatrical appearance and lose all efficacy and all semblance of holiness; hence, too, the ears of the people and even of many of the clergy no longer find the pleasure which the divine Word would give; hence a source of scandal for the good, little or no profit for the erring, who even when they crowd to hear fine language, drawn especially by big words about human progress, patriotism, recent discoveries of science, a hundred times repeated, punctuate the periods of the orator with prolonged applause, but leave the temple no better than they entered it, like those "who admired, but were not converted."[147]

This Sacred Congregation, therefore, wishing, by order of the Holy Father, to remove all these deadly abuses, obliges all the

[145] Card. Bausa Archiep. Florentin., *ad juniorem clerum*, 1893.

[146] *Ep.* 52 (2), *ad Nepotianum*, no. 8.

[147] St. Augustine, *In evangelium Joannis tractatus*, tract. 29, no. 2.

bishops and superiors general of religious communities and ecclesiastical institutes to employ all their apostolic zeal and energy to extirpate them.

Remembering the prescription of the Council of Trent, "they are to select men suitable for this office of preaching."[148] Let them perform this duty with the utmost zeal. In the case of priests of their own dioceses, the ordinaries must not admit them to this office until they have received a certificate of good life, knowledge, and conduct,[149] that is, until their capacity has been tested by an examination or in some other way. And in the case of priests from other dioceses, they must not allow them into the pulpit, especially on the principal solemnities, until they receive from their ordinary or religious superior a written attestation of their good conduct and of a sufficient preparation.

The superiors of all religious orders, societies, and congregations must not admit to the office of preaching, still less recommend to the ordinaries, any of their subjects until they have assured themselves of the upright life and suitable preparation for sacred oratory of the candidates. And if after having given letters of recommendation to a preacher, they find that his sermons are not in harmony with the directions given in this letter, they must at once call him to a sense of his duty, and if he refuse to obey, they must interdict him from the pulpit, even using, when necessary, the canonical penalties which the circumstances may require.

Exhortation to Renewed Vigilance

11. If we have thought it necessary to repeat and reproduce these prescriptions, ordering them to be religiously observed, the reason is that we are forced to it by the gravity of an evil which is increasing every day and which it would be extremely dangerous not to arrest immediately. For we have not now, as in the beginning, to deal with contradictors who present themselves in sheep's clothing, but with open and declared enemies—and in addition internal enemies,

[148] Session 5, *Decree on Reformation*, chap. 2.

[149] See Council of Trent, Session 5, *Decree on Reformation*, chap. 2.

who in alliance with the chief enemies of the Church are aiming at the ruin of the Faith. The audacity of these rises up each day against the wisdom which comes from heaven, arrogating to themselves the right to amend it as though it had become corrupted, to rejuvenate it as though it had become effete, to enlarge it and adapt it to the tendencies, progress, and interests of the age, as though it were opposed not to some superficial minds, but to the welfare of society.

Against these attacks on the teaching of the Gospel and Sacred Ecclesiastical Tradition those who have received the sacred Deposit of Faith can never offer too vigilant and severe an opposition.

As to the admonitions and prescriptions which, with certain knowledge, we have laid down in the present motu proprio, we will and ordain that they be religiously observed, both by all the ordinaries of the whole Catholic Church and by the superiors general of the regular orders and ecclesiastical institutes and that they be efficaciously applied, all things to the contrary notwithstanding.

Given at Rome at St. Peter's, September 1, 1910,
in the eighth year of Our Pontificate.

Orbem Catholicum

MOTU PROPRIO ON THE INSTITUTION OF CHRISTIAN DOCTRINE TO BE ORDERED THROUGHOUT THE CATHOLIC WORLD

Pope Pius XI

June 29, 1923

1. When we first addressed the Catholic world in Our encyclical letter,[150] we recalled that the only remedy for all the great ills that human society was suffering from was to seek the peace of Christ in the Kingdom of Christ: and we added that this kingdom on earth could not be established otherwise than by the work and industry of the Church, which is dedicated to educating men. This the Church does especially when, according to the wisdom of her institutions and laws, she imparts religious instruction to children and adults. For this reason, Our most beloved predecessor, Benedict XV, asked the Italian prelates, by letters issued by the Sacred Congregation of the Council, whether they were complying with the various prescriptions concerning the religious education of the people; to which questions they answered, each according to his own diligence and interest. Now, however, what the most vigilant pontiff had most opportunely begun, We, receiving this also with a willing heart as an inheritance handed down by him, have decided to complete. For the sake of this cause, and also so that we may extend the beneficial power of this undertaking to all nations, it pleases Us to undertake the plan of recalling the thoughts and studies of all good people to the cause of common salvation, and especially of assisting and strengthening the work and diligence of

[150] *Ubi arcano Dei consilio* (December 23, 1922).

the sacred pastors throughout the world in a matter in which nothing can be of greater interest, and of establishing a peculiar office at the Roman Curia, an office which will be called as such, by whose help we may better and more easily exercise the utmost vigilance and care which we owe to this great cause in the universal Church.

2. Therefore, by Our own motion and in the fullness of Our Apostolic power, We have instituted a peculiar office within the Sacred Congregation of the Council and declare it instituted by this letter, which the Apostolic See may use as an instrument to urge throughout the world the observance of its laws concerning the educating of the people in the precepts of the Christian doctrine: which office is to regulate and promote all catechetical activity in the Church.

3. Indeed, we are confident that salutary results will be obtained from it, especially if, as we do not doubt, the prompt and enthusiastic work of the bishops and other clergy and good laypeople, which they are accustomed to do, is added to the authority of the Apostolic See. However, if whatever an association and society of Catholics of both sexes would allow themselves to ask Us, in which field they may wish to gain ever more merits for the good of the Church, We would answer, that there seems to be neither more holy nor more necessary work for a Catholic faithful than to attend exemplarily the established sermons on catechism in their own parishes, or to serve as assistant in this matter to the parish clergy.

4. And we ask all the more earnestly that consecrated religious families of both sexes not only assist the individual bishops of their individual dioceses in this very matter, but also see to it that in their colleges the students are gradually instructed in catechism in such a way that, when they have perceived Christian doctrine more fully and wisely than they are accustomed to, and have been able to defend their faith against the things which are commonly objected

to, they may strive either to inculcate or to persuade others of the same faith.

5. We also greatly desire that in the principal seats of religious societies with the pastoral care for the youth, schools be opened, under the presidency and leadership of the bishops, for select youths of both sexes, who may be formed in an adapted course of study, and who, having passed the examination of their knowledge, may be duly declared fit to obtain the teaching degree of Christian doctrine and sacred and ecclesiastical history. Therefore, those who preside over religious houses should take care to choose from among their members those whom they wish to run such schools or to teach religious instruction to boys and girls.

6. It will be the duty of the bishops to constantly watch over all religious schools; and to report accurately to the Sacred Congregation of the Council every third year on the work undertaken in this field and on the outcome of the matter, especially as regards the higher schools and colleges, which we have mentioned. Thus, we hope, it will be fortunately done that the greatest stain of Catholic nations, which is ignorance of the divine religion, will be washed away, with the widespread return of thirsty souls to the inexhaustible fountains of truth and grace, that is, the water springing up into eternal life.

What We have established in these letters, We command to be always valid and firm, notwithstanding anything to the contrary.

Given at Rome at St. Peter's, on the twenty-ninth of June, the feast of the Prince of the Apostles, in the year 1923, the second of Our Pontificate.

Divini Illius Magistri

ENCYCLICAL ON THE CHRISTIAN EDUCATION OF YOUTH

Pope Pius XI

December 31, 1929

To the Patriarchs, Primates, Archbishops, Bishops, and other Ordinaries in Peace and Communion with the Apostolic See, and to All the Faithful of the Catholic World. Venerable Brethren and Beloved Children, Health and Apostolic Benediction.

1. Representative on earth of that divine Master Who, while embracing in the immensity of His love all mankind, even unworthy sinners, showed nevertheless a special tenderness and affection for children, and expressed Himself in those singularly touching words, "Suffer the little children to come unto Me" (Mk 10:14), We also on every occasion have endeavored to show the predilection wholly paternal which We bear toward them, particularly by Our assiduous care and timely instructions with reference to the Christian education of youth.

Reasons for Treating of Childhood Education

2. And so, in the spirit of the divine Master, We have directed a helpful word, now of admonition, now of exhortation, now of direction, to youths and to their educators, to fathers and mothers, on various points of Christian education, with that solicitude which becomes the common Father of all the Faithful, with an insistence in season and out of season, demanded by our pastoral office and inculcated by the apostle: "Be instant in season, out of season; reprove, entreat, rebuke in all patience and doctrine" (2 Tm 4:2).

Such insistence is called for in these our times, when, alas, there is so great and deplorable an absence of clear and sound principles, even regarding problems the most fundamental.

3. Now this same general condition of the times, this ceaseless agitation in various ways of the problem of educational rights and systems in different countries, the desire expressed to Us with filial confidence by not a few of yourselves, Venerable Brethren, and by members of your flocks, as well as Our deep affection toward youth above referred to, move Us to turn more directly to this subject, if not to treat it in all its well-nigh inexhaustible range of theory and practice, at least to summarize its main principles, throw full light on its important conclusions, and point out its practical applications.

4. Let this be the record of Our Sacerdotal Jubilee which, with altogether special affection, We wish to dedicate to our beloved youth, and to commend to all those whose office and duty is the work of education.

5. Indeed never has there been so much discussion about education as nowadays; never have exponents of new pedagogical theories been so numerous, or so many methods and means devised, proposed, and debated, not merely to facilitate education, but to create a new system infallibly efficacious, and capable of preparing the present generations for that earthly happiness which they so ardently desire.

6. The reason is that men, created by God to His image and likeness and destined for Him Who is infinite perfection, realize today more than ever, amid the most exuberant material progress, the insufficiency of earthly goods to produce true happiness, either for the individual or for the nations. And hence they feel more keenly in themselves the impulse toward a perfection that is higher, which

impulse is implanted in their rational nature by the Creator Himself. This perfection they seek to acquire by means of education. But many of them with, it would seem, too great insistence on the etymological meaning of the word, pretend to draw education out of human nature itself and evolve it by its own unaided powers. Such easily fall into error, because, instead of fixing their gaze on God, first principle and last end of the whole universe, they fall back upon themselves, becoming attached exclusively to passing things of earth; and thus their restlessness will never cease till they direct their attention and their efforts to God, the goal of all perfection, according to the profound saying of St. Augustine: "Thou didst create us, O Lord, for Thyself, and our heart is restless till it rest in Thee."[151]

Importance of Christian Education

7. It is therefore as important to make no mistake in education, as it is to make no mistake in the pursuit of the last end, with which the whole work of education is intimately and necessarily connected. In fact, since education consists essentially in preparing man for what he must be and for what he must do here below, in order to attain the sublime end for which he was created, it is clear that there can be no true education which is not wholly directed to man's last end, and that in the present order of Providence, since God has revealed Himself to us in the Person of His only begotten Son, Who alone is "the way, the truth, and the life" (Jn 14:6), there can be no ideally perfect education which is not Christian education.

8. From this we see the supreme importance of Christian education, not merely for each individual, but for families and for the whole of human society, whose perfection comes from the perfection of the elements that compose it. From these same principles, the excellence, we may well call it the unsurpassed excellence, of the work

[151] *Confessionum*, bk. 1, chap. 1.

of Christian education becomes manifest and clear; for after all it aims at securing the Supreme Good, that is, God, for the souls of those who are being educated, and the maximum of well-being possible here below for human society. And this it does as efficaciously as man is capable of doing it, namely, by cooperating with God in the perfecting of individuals and of society, inasmuch as education makes upon the soul the first, the most powerful and lasting impression for life according to the well-known saying of the wise man: "A young man according to his way, even when he is old, he will not depart from it" (Prv 22:6). With good reason therefore did St. John Chrysostom say, "What greater work is there than training the mind and forming the habits of the young?"[152]

9. But nothing discloses to us the supernatural beauty and excellence of the work of Christian education better than the sublime expression of love of Our Blessed Lord, identifying Himself with children: "Whosoever shall receive one such child as this in My name, receiveth Me" (Mk 9:36).

10. Now in order that no mistake be made in this work of utmost importance, and in order to conduct it in the best manner possible with the help of God's grace, it is necessary to have a clear and definite idea of Christian education in its essential aspects, viz., who has the mission to educate, who are the subjects to be educated, what are the necessary accompanying circumstances, what is the end and object proper to Christian education according to God's established order in the economy of His divine providence.

A Social Activity

11. Education is essentially a social and not a mere individual activity. Now there are three necessary societies, distinct from one another and yet harmoniously combined by God, into which man is born:

[152] *Hom.* 59 (60) *in Mattheum*, chap. 18, no. 7.

two, namely the family and civil society, belong to the natural order; the third, the Church, to the supernatural order.

12. In the first place comes the family, instituted directly by God for its peculiar purpose, the generation and formation of offspring; for this reason, it has priority of nature and therefore of rights over civil society. Nevertheless, the family is an imperfect society, since it has not in itself all the means for its own complete development; whereas civil society is a perfect society, having in itself all the means for its peculiar end, which is the temporal well-being of the community; and so, in this respect, that is, in view of the common good, it has preeminence over the family, which finds its own suitable temporal perfection precisely in civil society.

13. The third society, into which man is born when through baptism he reaches the divine life of grace, is the Church; a society of the supernatural order and of universal extent; a perfect society, because it has in itself all the means required for its own end, which is the eternal salvation of mankind; hence it is supreme in its own domain.

14. Consequently, education which is concerned with man as a whole, individually and socially, in the order of nature and in the order of grace, necessarily belongs to all these three societies, in due proportion, corresponding, according to the disposition of divine Providence, to the coordination of their respecting ends.

The Church

15. And first of all education belongs preeminently to the Church, by reason of a double title in the supernatural order, conferred exclusively upon her by God Himself; absolutely superior therefore to any other title in the natural order.

16. The first title is founded upon the express mission and supreme authority to teach, given her by her divine Founder: "All power is given to Me in heaven and in earth. Going therefore teach ye all nations, baptizing them in the name of the Father, and of the Son, and of the Holy Ghost, teaching them to observe all things whatsoever I have commanded you, and behold I am with you all days, even to the consummation of the world" (Mt 28:18–20). Upon this magisterial office Christ conferred infallibility, together with the command to teach His doctrine. Hence the Church "was set by her divine Author as the pillar and ground of truth, in order to teach the divine Faith to men, and keep whole and inviolate the deposit confided to her; to direct and fashion men, in all their actions individually and socially, to purity of morals and integrity of life, in accordance with revealed doctrine."[153]

Supernatural Motherhood

17. The second title is the supernatural motherhood, in virtue of which the Church, spotless Spouse of Christ, generates, nurtures, and educates souls in the divine life of grace, with her sacraments and her doctrine. With good reason then does St. Augustine maintain: "He has not God for Father who refuses to have the Church as mother."[154]

18. Hence it is that in this proper object of her mission, that is, "in faith and morals, God Himself has made the Church sharer in the divine Magisterium and, by a special privilege, granted her immunity from error; hence she is the mistress of men, supreme and absolutely sure, and she has inherent in herself an inviolable right to

[153] Pope Pius IX, *Quum non sine.*

[154] St. Cyprian, *De unitate ecclesiae*, no. 6. Editor's Note: This famous quotation was originally cited as coming from St. Augustine's *Sermo de symbolo ad catechumenos*, cf. no. 1: "But ye begin to have Him for your Father, when you have been born by the Church as your mother."

freedom in teaching."[155] By necessary consequence the Church is independent of any sort of earthly power as well in the origin as in the exercise of her mission as educator, not merely in regard to her proper end and object, but also in regard to the means necessary and suitable to attain that end. Hence, with regard to every other kind of human learning and instruction, which is the common patrimony of individuals and society, the Church has an independent right to make use of it, and, above all, to decide what may help or harm Christian education. And this must be so, because the Church as a perfect society has an independent right to the means conducive to its end, and because every form of instruction, no less than every human action, has a necessary connection with man's last end, and therefore cannot be withdrawn from the dictates of the divine law, of which the Church is guardian, interpreter, and infallible mistress.

19. This truth is clearly set forth by Pius X of saintly memory: "Whatever a Christian does even in the order of things of earth, he may not overlook the supernatural; indeed he must, according to the teaching of Christian wisdom, direct all things toward the supreme good as to his last end; all his actions, besides, insofar as good or evil in the order of morality, that is, in keeping or not with natural and divine law, fall under the judgment and jurisdiction of the Church."[156]

20. It is worthy of note how a layman, an excellent writer and at the same time a profound and conscientious thinker, has been able to understand well and express exactly this fundamental Catholic doctrine:

> The Church does not say that morality belongs purely, in the sense of exclusively, to her; but that it belongs wholly to her. She has

[155] Pope Leo XIII, Encyclical *Libertas* (June 20, 1888), no. 27.
[156] Encyclical *Singulari quadam* (September 24, 1912), no. 3.

never maintained that, outside her fold and apart from her teaching, man cannot arrive at any moral truth; she has on the contrary more than once condemned this opinion because it has appeared under more forms than one. She does, however, say, has said, and will ever say, that because of her institution by Jesus Christ, because of the Holy Ghost sent her in His name by the Father, she alone possesses what she has had immediately from God and can never lose: the whole of moral truth, *omnem veritatem*, in which all individual moral truths are included, as well those which man may learn by the help of reason, as those which form part of revelation or which may be deduced from it.[157]

The Rights of the Church

21. Therefore with full right the Church promotes letters, science, art insofar as necessary or helpful to Christian education, in addition to her work for the salvation of souls: founding and maintaining schools and institutions adapted to every branch of learning and degree of culture.[158] Nor may even physical culture, as it is called, be considered outside the range of her maternal supervision, for the reason that it also is a means which may help or harm Christian education.

22. And this work of the Church in every branch of culture is of immense benefit to families and nations which without Christ are lost, as St. Hilary points out correctly: "What can be more fraught with danger for the world than the rejection of Christ?"[159] Nor does it interfere in the least with the regulations of the State, because the Church in her motherly prudence is not unwilling that her schools and institutions for the education of the laity be in keeping with the legitimate dispositions of civil authority; she is in every way ready to cooperate with this authority and to make provision for a mutual understanding, should difficulties arise.

[157] Alessandro Manzoni, *Osservazioni sulla Morale Cattolica*, pt. 1, chap. 3.
[158] See *Code of Canon Law* [1917], can. 1375.
[159] *In Mattheum*, chap. 18.

23. Again, it is the inalienable right as well as the indispensable duty of the Church to watch over the entire education of her children, in all institutions, public or private, not merely in regard to the religious instruction there given, but in regard to every other branch of learning and every regulation insofar as religion and morality are concerned.[160]

24. Nor should the exercise of this right be considered undue interference, but rather maternal care on the part of the Church in protecting her children from the grave danger of all kinds of doctrinal and moral evil. Moreover, this watchfulness of the Church not merely can create no real inconvenience, but must on the contrary confer valuable assistance in the right ordering and well-being of families and of civil society; for it keeps far away from youth the moral poison which at that inexperienced and changeable age more easily penetrates the mind and more rapidly spreads its baneful effects. For it is true, as Leo XIII has wisely pointed out, that, without proper religious and moral instruction, "every form of intellectual culture will be injurious; for young people not accustomed to respect God will be unable to bear the restraint of a virtuous life, and, never having learned to deny themselves anything, they will easily be incited to disturb the public order."[161]

THE CHURCH'S MISSION

25. The extent of the Church's mission in the field of education is such as to embrace every nation, without exception, according to the command of Christ: "Teach ye all nations" (Mt 28:19); and there is no power on earth that may lawfully oppose her or stand in her way. In the first place, it extends over all the faithful, of whom she has anxious care as a tender mother. For these she has throughout the centuries created and conducted an immense number of

[160] See *Code of Canon Law* [1917], cann. 1381, 1382.
[161] *Nobilissima Gallorum*, no. 3.

schools and institutions in every branch of learning. As We said on a recent occasion:

> Right back in the far-off Middle Ages, when there were so many (some have even said too many) monasteries, convents, churches, collegiate churches, cathedral chapters, etc., there was attached to each a home of study, of teaching, of Christian education. To these we must add all the universities, spread over every country and always by the initiative and under the protection of the Holy See and the Church. That grand spectacle, which today we see better, as it is nearer to us and more imposing because of the conditions of the age, was the spectacle of all times; and they who study and compare historical events remain astounded at what the Church has been able to do in this matter, and marvel at the manner in which she had succeeded in fulfilling her God-given mission to educate generations of men to a Christian life, producing everywhere a magnificent harvest of fruitful results. But if we wonder that the Church in all times has been able to gather about her and educate hundreds, thousands, millions of students, no less wonderful is it to bear in mind what she has done not only in the field of education, but in that also of true and genuine erudition. For, if so many treasures of culture, civilization, and literature have escaped destruction, this is due to the action by which the Church, even in times long past and uncivilized, has shed so bright a light in the domain of letters, of philosophy, of art, and, in a special manner, of architecture.[162]

26. All this the Church has been able to do because her mission to educate extends equally to those outside the fold, seeing that all men are called to enter the Kingdom of God and reach eternal salvation. Just as today when her missions scatter schools by the thousand in districts and countries not yet Christian, from the banks of the Ganges to the Yellow River and the great islands and archipelagos of the

[162] Pope Pius XI, Discourse to the students of Mondragone College (May 14, 1929).

Pacific Ocean, from the Dark Continent to the Land of Fire and to frozen Alaska, so in every age the Church by her missionaries has educated to Christian life and to civilization the various peoples which now constitute the Christian nations of the civilized world.

27. Hence it is evident that both by right and in fact the mission to educate belongs preeminently to the Church, and that no one free from prejudice can have a reasonable motive for opposing or impeding the Church in this her work, of which the world today enjoys the precious advantages.

The Family and the State

28. This is the more true because the rights of the family and of the State, even the rights of individuals regarding a just liberty in the pursuit of science, of methods of science, and all sorts of profane culture, not only are not opposed to this preeminence of the Church, but are in complete harmony with it. The fundamental reason for this harmony is that the supernatural order, to which the Church owes her rights, not only does not in the least destroy the natural order, to which pertain the other rights mentioned, but elevates the natural and perfects it, each affording mutual aid to the other, and completing it in a manner proportioned to its respective nature and dignity. The reason is because both come from God, Who cannot contradict Himself: "The works of God are perfect and all His ways are judgments" (Dt 32:4).

29. This becomes clearer when we consider more closely and in detail the mission of education proper to the family and to the State.

The Family

30. In the first place, the Church's mission of education is in wonderful agreement with that of the family, for both proceed from God, and in a remarkably similar manner. God directly communicates to the

family, in the natural order, fecundity, which is the principle of life, and hence also the principle of education to life, together with authority, the principle of order.

31. The Angelic Doctor, with his wonted clearness of thought and precision of style, says: "The father according to the flesh has in a particular way a share in that principle which in a manner universal is found in God. The father is the principle of generation, of education and discipline, and of everything that bears upon the perfecting of human life."[163]

32. The family therefore holds directly from the Creator the mission and hence the right to educate the offspring, a right inalienable because inseparably joined to the strict obligation, a right anterior to any right whatever of civil society and of the State, and therefore inviolable on the part of any power on earth.

33. That this right is inviolable St. Thomas proves as follows: "The child is naturally something of the father ... so by natural right the child, before reaching the use of reason, is under the father's care. Hence it would be contrary to natural justice if the child, before the use of reason, were removed from the care of its parents, or if any disposition were made concerning him against the will of the parents."[164] And as this duty on the part of the parents continues up to the time when the child is in a position to provide for itself, this same inviolable parental right of education also endures. "Nature intends not merely the generation of the offspring, but also its development and advance to the perfection of man considered as man, that is, to the state of virtue," says the same St. Thomas.[165]

[163] ST, II-II, q. 102, a. 1, c.
[164] ST, II-II, q. 10, a. 12, c.
[165] ST, III-Sup., q. 41, a. 1, c.

34. The wisdom of the Church in this matter is expressed with precision and clearness in the Codex of Canon Law, can. 1113: "Parents are under a grave obligation to see to the religious and moral education of their children, as well as to their physical and civic training, as far as they can, and moreover to provide for their temporal well-being."

35. On this point the common sense of mankind is in such complete accord, that they would be in open contradiction with it who dared maintain that the children belong to the State before they belong to the family, and that the State has an absolute right over their education. Untenable is the reason they adduce, namely, that man is born a citizen and hence belongs primarily to the State, not bearing in mind that before being a citizen man must exist; and existence does not come from the State, but from the parents, as Leo XIII wisely declared: "The children are something of the father, and as it were an extension of the person of the father; and, to be perfectly accurate, they enter into and become part of civil society, not directly by themselves, but through the family in which they were born."[166] "And therefore," says the same Leo XIII, "the father's power is of such a nature that it cannot be destroyed or absorbed by the State; for it has the same origin as human life itself."[167]

Not Despotic

It does not however follow from this that the parents' right to educate their children is absolute and despotic; for it is necessarily subordinated to the last end and to natural and divine law, as Leo XIII declares in another memorable encyclical, where He thus sums up the rights and duties of parents:

> By nature, parents have a right to the training of their children, but with this added duty: that the education and instruction of the

[166] Encyclical *Rerum novarum* (May 15, 1891), no. 14.
[167] *Rerum novarum*, no. 14.

child be in accord with the end for which, by God's blessing, it was begotten. Therefore, it is the duty of parents to make every effort to prevent any invasion of their rights in this matter, and to make absolutely sure that the education of their children remain under their own control in keeping with their Christian duty, and above all to refuse to send them to those schools in which there is danger of imbibing the deadly poison of impiety.[168]

36. It must be borne in mind also that the obligation of the family to bring up children includes not only religious and moral education, but physical and civic education as well,[169] principally insofar as it touches upon religion and morality.

37. This incontestable right of the family has at various times been recognized by nations anxious to respect the natural law in their civil enactments. Thus, to give one recent example, the Supreme Court of the United States of America, in a decision on an important controversy, declared that it is not in the competence of the State to fix any uniform standard of education by forcing children to receive instruction exclusively in public schools, and it bases its decision on the natural law: the child is not the mere creature of the State; those who nurture him and direct his destiny have the right, coupled with the high duty, to educate him and prepare him for the fulfillment of his obligations.[170]

[168] Encyclical *Sapientiae Christianae* (January 10, 1890), no. 42.

[169] See *Code of Canon Law* [1917], can. 1113.

[170] "The fundamental theory of liberty upon which all governments in this Union repose excludes any general power of the State to standardize its children by forcing them to accept instruction from public teachers only. The child is not the mere creature of the State; those who nurture him and direct his destiny have the right, coupled with the high duty, to recognize and prepare him for additional duties." U. S. Supreme Court Decision in the Oregon School Case (June 1, 1925).

Tutelage of the Church

38. History bears witness how, particularly in modern times, the State has violated and does violate rights conferred by God on the family. At the same time, it shows magnificently how the Church has ever protected and defended these rights, a fact proved by the special confidence which parents have in Catholic schools. As We pointed out recently in Our Letter to the Cardinal Secretary of State: "The family has instinctively understood this to be so, and from the earliest days of Christianity down to our own times, fathers and mothers, even those of little or no faith, have been sending or bringing their children in millions to places of education under the direction of the Church."[171]

39. It is paternal instinct, given by God, that thus turns with confidence to the Church, certain of finding in her the protection of family rights, thereby illustrating that harmony with which God has ordered all things. The Church is indeed conscious of her divine mission to all mankind, and of the obligation which all men have to practice the one true religion; and therefore she never tires of defending her right, and of reminding parents of their duty, to have all Catholic-born children baptized and brought up as Christians. On the other hand, so jealous is she of the family's inviolable natural right to educate the children, that she never consents, save under peculiar circumstances and with special cautions, to baptize the children of infidels, or provide for their education against the will of the parents, till such time as the children can choose for themselves and freely embrace the Faith.[172]

40. We have therefore two facts of supreme importance. As We said in Our discourse cited above: "The Church placing at the disposal of

[171] May 30, 1929, in *Acta Apostolicae Sedis* [AAS], 21:302.

[172] See *Code of Canon Law* [1917], can. 750, § 2; and St. Thomas Aquinas, ST, II-II, q. 10, a. 12.

families her office of mistress and educator, and the families eager to profit by the offer, and entrusting their children to the Church in hundreds and thousands. These two facts recall and proclaim a striking truth of the greatest significance in the moral and social order. They declare that the mission of education regards before all, above all, primarily the Church and the family, and this by natural and divine law, and that therefore it cannot be slighted, cannot be evaded, cannot be supplanted."[173]

State Rights

41. From such priority of rights on the part of the Church and of the family in the field of education, most important advantages, as we have seen, accrue to the whole of society. Moreover, in accordance with the divinely established order of things, no damage can follow from it to the true and just rights of the State in regard to the education of its citizens.

42. These rights have been conferred upon civil society by the Author of nature Himself, not by title of fatherhood, as in the case of the Church and of the family, but in virtue of the authority which it possesses to promote the common temporal welfare, which is precisely the purpose of its existence. Consequently, education cannot pertain to civil society in the same way in which it pertains to the Church and to the family, but in a different way corresponding to its own particular end and object.

43. Now this end and object, the common welfare in the temporal order, consists in that peace and security in which families and individual citizens have the free exercise of their rights, and at the same time enjoy the greatest spiritual and temporal prosperity possible in this life, by the mutual union and coordination of the work of all.

[173] Pope Pius XI, Discourse to the students of Mondragone College (May 14, 1929).

The function therefore of the civil authority residing in the State is twofold: to protect and to foster, but by no means to absorb the family and the individual, or to substitute itself for them.

44. Accordingly, in the matter of education, it is the right, or to speak more correctly, it is the duty of the State to protect in its legislation, the prior rights, already described, of the family as regards the Christian education of its offspring, and consequently also to respect the supernatural rights of the Church in this same realm of Christian education.

45. It also belongs to the State to protect the rights of the child itself when the parents are found wanting either physically or morally in this respect, whether by default, incapacity, or misconduct, since, as has been shown, their right to educate is not an absolute and despotic one, but dependent on the natural and divine law, and therefore subject alike to the authority and jurisdiction of the Church, and to the vigilance and administrative care of the State in view of the common good. Besides, the family is not a perfect society, that is, it has not in itself all the means necessary for its full development. In such cases, exceptional no doubt, the State does not put itself in the place of the family, but merely supplies deficiencies, and provides suitable means, always in conformity with the natural rights of the child and the supernatural rights of the Church.

46. In general, then, it is the right and duty of the State to protect, according to the rules of right reason and faith, the moral and religious education of youth, by removing public impediments that stand in the way.

Instruction of Youth

In the first place it pertains to the State, in view of the common good, to promote in various ways the education and instruction of youth. It should begin by encouraging and assisting, of its own accord, the initiative and activity of the Church and the family, whose successes in this field have been clearly demonstrated by history and experience. It should moreover supplement their work whenever this falls short of what is necessary, even by means of its own schools and institutions. For the State more than any other society is provided with the means put at its disposal for the needs of all, and it is only right that it use these means to the advantage of those who have contributed them.[174]

47. Over and above this, the State can exact and take measures to secure that all its citizens have the necessary knowledge of their civic and political duties, and a certain degree of physical, intellectual, and moral culture, which, considering the conditions of our times, is really necessary for the common good.

48. However, it is clear that in all these ways of promoting education and instruction, both public and private, the State should respect the inherent rights of the Church and of the family concerning Christian education, and moreover have regard for distributive justice. Accordingly, unjust and unlawful is any monopoly, educational or scholastic, which, physically or morally, forces families to make use of government schools, contrary to the dictates of their Christian conscience, or contrary even to their legitimate preferences.

49. This does not prevent the State from making due provision for the right administration of public affairs and for the protection of its peace, within or without the realm. These are things which directly concern the public good and call for special aptitudes and special preparation. The State may therefore reserve to itself the establish-

[174] See Pope Pius XI, Discourse to the students of Mondragone College (May 14, 1929).

ment and direction of schools intended to prepare for certain civic duties and especially for military service, provided it be careful not to injure the rights of the Church or of the family in what pertains to them. It is well to repeat this warning here; for in these days there is spreading a spirit of nationalism which is false and exaggerated, as well as dangerous to true peace and prosperity. Under its influence various excesses are committed in giving a military turn to the so-called physical training of boys (sometimes even of girls, contrary to the very instincts of human nature); or again in usurping unreasonably on Sunday, the time which should be devoted to religious duties and to family life at home. It is not Our intention however to condemn what is good in the spirit of discipline and legitimate bravery promoted by these methods; We condemn only what is excessive, as for example violence, which must not be confounded with courage nor with the noble sentiment of military valor in defense of country and public order; or again exaltation of athleticism which even in classic pagan times marked the decline and downfall of genuine physical training.

50. In general, also, it belongs to civil society and the State to provide what may be called civic education, not only for its youth, but for all ages and classes. This consists in the practice of presenting publicly to groups of individuals information having an intellectual, imaginative, and emotional appeal, calculated to draw their wills to what is upright and honest, and to urge its practice by a sort of moral compulsion, positively by disseminating such knowledge, and negatively by suppressing what is opposed to it.[175] This civic education, so wide and varied in itself as to include almost every activity of the State intended for the public good, ought also to be regulated by the norms of rectitude, and therefore cannot conflict

[175] Luigi Taparelli, *Saggio teoretico di diritto naturale appogiato sul fatto*, rev. ed. (Rome, 1855), no. 922; a work never sufficiently praised and recommended to university students (see Our Discourse of December 18, 1927).

with the doctrines of the Church, which is the divinely appointed teacher of these norms.

Church and State

51. All that we have said so far regarding the activity of the State in educational matters rests on the solid and immovable foundation of the Catholic doctrine of *The Christian Constitution of States* set forth in such masterly fashion by Our predecessor, Leo XIII, notably in the Encyclicals *Immortale Dei*[176] and *Sapientiae Christianae*.[177] He writes as follows:

> God has divided the government of the human race between two authorities, ecclesiastical and civil, establishing one over things divine, the other over things human. Both are supreme, each in its own domain; each has its own fixed boundaries which limit its activities. These boundaries are determined by the peculiar nature and the proximate end of each, and describe as it were a sphere within which, with exclusive right, each may develop its influence. As however the same subjects are under the two authorities, it may happen that the same matter, though from a different point of view, may come under the competence and jurisdiction of each of them. It follows that divine Providence, whence both authorities have their origin, must have traced with due order the proper line of action for each. "The powers that are, are ordained of God" (Rom 13:1).[178]

52. Now the education of youth is precisely one of those matters that belong both to the Church and to the State, "though in different ways," as explained above.

> Therefore—continues Leo XIII—between the two powers there must reign a well-ordered harmony. Not without reason may this mutual agreement be compared to the union of body and soul in

[176] November 1, 1885.
[177] January 10, 1890.
[178] Pope Leo XIII, *Immortale Dei*, no. 6.

man. Its nature and extent can only be determined by considering, as we have said, the nature of each of the two powers and, in particular, the excellence and nobility of the respective ends. To one is committed directly and specifically the charge of what is helpful in worldly matters; while the other is to concern itself with the things that pertain to heaven and eternity. Everything therefore in human affairs that is in any way sacred, or has reference to the salvation of souls and the worship of God, whether by its nature or by its end, is subject to the jurisdiction and discipline of the Church. Whatever else is comprised in the civil and political order, rightly comes under the authority of the State; for Christ commanded us to give to Caesar the things that are Caesar's, and to God the things that are God's.[179]

53. Whoever refuses to admit these principles, and hence to apply them to education, must necessarily deny that Christ has founded His Church for the eternal salvation of mankind, and maintain instead that civil society and the State are not subject to God and to His law, natural and divine. Such a doctrine is manifestly impious, contrary to right reason, and, especially in this matter of education, extremely harmful to the proper training of youth, and disastrous as well for civil society as for the well-being of all mankind. On the other hand, from the application of these principles, there inevitably result immense advantages for the right formation of citizens. This is abundantly proved by the history of every age. Tertullian in his *Apologeticus* could throw down a challenge to the enemies of the Church in the early days of Christianity, just as St. Augustine did in his; and we today can repeat with him:

> Let those who declare the teaching of Christ to be opposed to the welfare of the State furnish us with an army of soldiers such as Christ says soldiers ought to be; let them give us subjects, husbands, wives, parents, children, masters, servants, kings, judges, taxpayers, and tax gatherers who live up to the teachings of Christ; and then

[179] *Immortale Dei*, no. 6.

let them dare assert that Christian doctrine is harmful to the State. Rather let them not hesitate one moment to acclaim that doctrine, rightly observed, the greatest safeguard of the State.[180]

54. While treating of education, it is not out of place to show here how an ecclesiastical writer, who flourished in more recent times, during the Renaissance, the holy and learned Cardinal Silvio Antoniano, to whom the cause of Christian education is greatly indebted, has set forth most clearly this well-established point of Catholic doctrine. He had been a disciple of that wonderful educator of youth, St. Philip Neri; he was teacher and Latin secretary to St. Charles Borromeo, and it was at the latter's suggestion and under his inspiration that he wrote his splendid treatise on *The Christian Education of Youth*. In it he argues as follows:

True Harmony

The more closely the temporal power of a nation aligns itself with the spiritual, and the more it fosters and promotes the latter, by so much the more it contributes to the conservation of the commonwealth. For it is the aim of the ecclesiastical authority, by the use of spiritual means, to form good Christians in accordance with its own particular end and object; and, in doing this, it helps at the same time to form good citizens, and prepares them to meet their obligations as members of a civil society. This follows of necessity because in the City of God, the holy Roman Catholic Church, a good citizen and an upright man are absolutely one and the same thing. How grave therefore is the error of those who separate things so closely united, and who think that they can produce good citizens by ways and methods other than those which make for the formation of good Christians. For, let human prudence say what it likes and reason as it pleases, it is impossible to produce true temporal peace and tranquility by things repugnant or opposed to the peace and happiness of eternity.[181]

[180] St. Augustine, *Ep.* 138, chap. 2, no. 15.

[181] Cardinal Silvio Antoniano, *Tre libri dell' educazione cristiana de' figliuoli* (Verona, 1583), bk. 1, chap. 43.

55. What is true of the State, is true also of science, scientific methods, and scientific research; they have nothing to fear from the full and perfect mandate which the Church holds in the field of education. Our Catholic institutions, whatever their grade in the educational and scientific world, have no need of apology. The esteem they enjoy, the praise they receive, the learned works which they promote and produce in such abundance, and above all, the men, fully and splendidly equipped, whom they provide for the magistracy, for the professions, for the teaching career, in fact for every walk of life, more than sufficiently testify in their favor.[182]

56. These facts moreover present a most striking confirmation of the Catholic doctrine defined by the Vatican Council:

> Not only is it impossible for faith and reason to be at variance with each other, they are on the contrary of mutual help. For while right reason establishes the foundations of faith, and, by the help of its light, develops a knowledge of the things of God, faith on the other hand frees and preserves reason from error and enriches it with varied knowledge. The Church, therefore, far from hindering the pursuit of the arts and sciences, fosters and promotes them in many ways. For she is neither ignorant nor unappreciative of the many advantages which flow from them to mankind. On the contrary, she admits that, just as they come from God, Lord of all knowledge, so too if rightly used, with the help of His grace, they lead to God. Nor does she prevent the sciences, each in its own sphere, from making use of principles and methods of their own. Only while acknowledging the freedom due to them, she takes every precaution to prevent them from falling into error by opposition to divine doctrine, or from overstepping their proper limits, and thus invading and disturbing the domain of faith.[183]

[182] See Pope Pius XI, Letter to the Cardinal Secretary of State (May 30, 1929), in AAS, 21:297–306.

[183] Council of Vatican I, Session 3, chap. 4.

57. This norm of a just freedom in things scientific serves also as an inviolable norm of a just freedom in things didactic, or for rightly understood liberty in teaching; it should be observed therefore in whatever instruction is imparted to others. Its obligation is all the more binding in justice when there is question of instructing youth. For in this work, the teacher, whether public or private, has no absolute right of his own, but only such as has been communicated to him by others. Besides, every Christian child or youth has a strict right to instruction in harmony with the teaching of the Church, the pillar and ground of truth. And whoever disturbs the pupil's faith in any way does him grave wrong, inasmuch as he abuses the trust which children place in their teachers, and takes unfair advantage of their inexperience and of their natural craving for unrestrained liberty, at once illusory and false.

Subject of Education

58. In fact, it must never be forgotten that the subject of Christian education is man whole and entire, soul united to body in unity of nature, with all his faculties natural and supernatural, such as right reason and revelation show him to be; man, therefore, fallen from his original estate, but redeemed by Christ and restored to the supernatural condition of adopted son of God, though without the preternatural privileges of bodily immortality or perfect control of appetite. There remain, therefore, in human nature the effects of Original Sin, the chief of which are weakness of will and disorderly inclinations.

59. "Folly is bound up in the heart of a child, and the rod of correction shall drive it away" (Prv 22:15). Disorderly inclinations then must be corrected, good tendencies encouraged and regulated from tender childhood, and, above all, the mind must be enlightened and the will strengthened by supernatural truth and by the means of grace, without which it is impossible to control evil im-

pulses, impossible to attain to the full and complete perfection of education intended by the Church, which Christ has endowed so richly with divine doctrine and with the sacraments, the efficacious means of grace.

False Naturalism

60. Hence every form of pedagogic naturalism which in any way excludes or weakens supernatural Christian formation in the teaching of youth is false. Every method of education founded, wholly or in part, on the denial or forgetfulness of Original Sin and of grace, and relying on the sole powers of human nature, is unsound. Such, generally speaking, are those modern systems bearing various names which appeal to a pretended self-government and unrestrained freedom on the part of the child, and which diminish or even suppress the teacher's authority and action, attributing to the child an exclusive primacy of initiative, and an activity independent of any higher law, natural or divine, in the work of his education.

61. If any of these terms are used, less properly, to denote the necessity of a gradually more active cooperation on the part of the pupil in his own education; if the intention is to banish from education despotism and violence—which, by the way, just punishment is not—this would be correct, but in no way new. It would mean only what has been taught and reduced to practice by the Church in traditional Christian education, in imitation of the method employed by God Himself toward His creatures, of whom He demands active cooperation according to the nature of each; for His Wisdom "reacheth from end to end mightily and ordereth all things sweetly" (Ws 8:1).

62. But alas! it is clear from the obvious meaning of the words and from experience, that what is intended by not a few is the withdrawal of education from every sort of dependence on the divine

law. So today we see, strange sight indeed, educators and philosophers who spend their lives in searching for a universal moral code of education, as if there existed no Decalogue, no Gospel law, no law even of nature stamped by God on the heart of man, promulgated by right reason, and codified in positive revelation by God Himself in the Ten Commandments. These innovators are wont to refer contemptuously to Christian education as "heteronomous," "passive," "obsolete," because founded upon the authority of God and His holy law.

63. Such men are miserably deluded in their claim to emancipate, as they say, the child, while in reality they are making him the slave of his own blind pride and of his disorderly affections, which, as a logical consequence of this false system, come to be justified as legitimate demands of a so-called autonomous nature.

64. But what is worse is the claim, not only vain but false, irreverent, and dangerous, to submit to research, experiment, and conclusions of a purely natural and profane order, those matters of education which belong to the supernatural order; as, for example, questions of priestly or religious vocation, and in general the secret workings of grace which indeed elevate the natural powers, but are infinitely superior to them, and may nowise be subjected to physical laws, for "the Spirit breatheth where He will" (Jn 3:8).

Sex Instruction

65. Another very grave danger is that naturalism which nowadays invades the field of education in that most delicate matter of purity of morals. Far too common is the error of those who with dangerous assurance and under an ugly term propagate a so-called sex education, falsely imagining they can forearm youths against the dangers of sensuality by means purely natural, such as a foolhardy initiation and precautionary instruction for all indiscriminately, even

in public; and, worse still, by exposing them at an early age to the occasions, in order to accustom them, so it is argued, and as it were to harden them against such dangers.

66. Such persons grievously err in refusing to recognize the inborn weakness of human nature, and the law of which the apostle speaks, fighting against the law of the mind (see Rom 7:23); and also in ignoring the experience of facts, from which it is clear that, particularly in young people, evil practices are the effect not so much of ignorance of intellect as of weakness of a will exposed to dangerous occasions, and unsupported by the means of grace.

67. In this extremely delicate matter, if, all things considered, some private instruction is found necessary and opportune, from those who hold from God the commission to teach and who have the grace of state, every precaution must be taken. Such precautions are well known in traditional Christian education, and are adequately described by Antoniano cited above, when he says:

> Such is our misery and inclination to sin, that often in the very things considered to be remedies against sin, we find occasions for and inducements to sin itself. Hence it is of the highest importance that a good father, while discussing with his son a matter so delicate, should be well on his guard and not descend to details, nor refer to the various ways in which this infernal hydra destroys with its poison so large a portion of the world; otherwise, it may happen that, instead of extinguishing this fire, he unwittingly stirs or kindles it in the simple and tender heart of the child. Speaking generally, during the period of childhood, it suffices to employ those remedies which produce the double effect of opening the door to the virtue of purity and closing the door upon vice.[184]

[184] Cardinal Silvio Antoniano, *Tre libri dell' educazione cristiana de' figliuoli*, bk. 2, chap. 88.

Coeducation

68. False also and harmful to Christian education is the so-called method of "coeducation." This too, by many of its supporters, is founded upon naturalism and the denial of Original Sin; but by all, upon a deplorable confusion of ideas that mistakes a leveling promiscuity and equality, for the legitimate association of the sexes. The Creator has ordained and disposed perfect union of the sexes only in matrimony, and, with varying degrees of contact, in the family and in society. Besides, there is not in nature itself, which fashions the two quite different in organism, in temperament, in abilities, anything to suggest that there can be or ought to be promiscuity, and much less equality, in the training of the two sexes. These, in keeping with the wonderful designs of the Creator, are destined to complement each other in the family and in society, precisely because of their differences, which therefore ought to be maintained and encouraged during their years of formation, with the necessary distinction and corresponding separation, according to age and circumstances. These principles, with due regard to time and place, must, in accordance with Christian prudence, be applied to all schools, particularly in the most delicate and decisive period of formation, that, namely, of adolescence; and in gymnastic exercises and deportment, special care must be had of Christian modesty in young women and girls, which is so gravely impaired by any kind of exhibition in public.

69. Recalling the terrible words of the divine Master, "Woe to the world because of scandals!" (Mt 18:7), We most earnestly appeal to your solicitude and your watchfulness, Venerable Brethren, against these pernicious errors, which, to the immense harm of youth, are spreading far and wide among Christian peoples.

70. In order to obtain perfect education, it is of the utmost importance to see that all those conditions which surround the child during

the period of his formation, in other words, that the combination of circumstances which we call "environment," correspond exactly to the end proposed.

The Christian Family

71. The first natural and necessary element in this environment, as regards education, is the family, and this precisely because so ordained by the Creator Himself. Accordingly, that education, as a rule, will be more effective and lasting which is received in a well-ordered and well-disciplined Christian family; and more efficacious in proportion to the clear and constant good example set, first by the parents, and then by the other members of the household.

72. It is not our intention to treat formally the question of domestic education, nor even to touch upon its principal points. The subject is too vast. Besides, there are not lacking special treatises on this topic by authors, both ancient and modern, well known for their solid Catholic doctrine. One which seems deserving of special mention is the golden treatise already referred to, of Antoniano, *On the Christian Education of Youth,* which St. Charles Borromeo ordered to be read in public to parents assembled in their churches.

73. Nevertheless, Venerable Brethren and beloved children, We wish to call your attention in a special manner to the present-day lamentable decline in family education. The offices and professions of a transitory and earthly life, which are certainly of far less importance, are prepared for by long and careful study; whereas, for the fundamental duty and obligation of educating their children, many parents have little or no preparation, immersed as they are in temporal cares. The declining influence of domestic environment is further weakened by another tendency, prevalent almost everywhere today, which, under one pretext or another, for economic reasons, or for reasons of industry, trade, or politics, causes chil-

dren to be more and more frequently sent away from home even in their tenderest years. And there is a country where the children are actually being torn from the bosom of the family, to be formed (or, to speak more accurately, to be deformed and depraved) in godless schools and associations, to irreligion and hatred, according to the theories of advanced socialism; and thus is renewed in a real and more terrible manner the slaughter of the Innocents.

Obligation of Parents

74. For the love of Our Savior, Jesus Christ, therefore, we implore pastors of souls, by every means in their power, by instructions and catechisms, by word of mouth and written articles widely distributed, to warn Christian parents of their grave obligations. And this should be done not in a merely theoretical and general way, but with practical and specific application to the various responsibilities of parents touching the religious, moral, and civil training of their children, and with indication of the methods best adapted to make their training effective, supposing always the influence of their own exemplary lives. The Apostle of the Gentiles did not hesitate to descend to such details of practical instruction in his epistles, especially in the Epistle to the Ephesians, where among other things he gives this advice: "And you, fathers, provoke not your children to anger" (6:4). This fault is the result not so much of excessive severity, as of impatience and of ignorance of means best calculated to effect a desired correction; it is also due to the all-too-common relaxation of parental discipline which fails to check the growth of evil passions in the hearts of the younger generation. Parents, therefore, and all who take their place in the work of education, should be careful to make right use of the authority given them by God, Whose vicars in a true sense they are. This authority is not given for their own advantage, but for the proper upbringing of their children in a holy and filial "fear of God, the beginning of wisdom" (Ecclus 1:16), on which foundation alone all respect for authority can rest securely;

and without which, order, tranquility, and prosperity, whether in the family or in society, will be impossible.

Educational Environment

75. To meet the weakness of man's fallen nature, God in His goodness has provided the abundant helps of His grace and the countless means with which He has endowed the Church, the great family of Christ. The Church therefore is the educational environment most intimately and harmoniously associated with the Christian family.

76. This educational environment of the Church embraces the sacraments, divinely efficacious means of grace, the sacred ritual, so wonderfully instructive, and the material fabric of her churches, whose liturgy and art have an immense educational value; but it also includes the great number and variety of schools, associations, and institutions of all kinds, established for the training of youth in Christian piety, together with literature and the sciences, not omitting recreation and physical culture. And in this inexhaustible fecundity of educational works, how marvelous, how incomparable is the Church's maternal providence! So admirable too is the harmony which she maintains with the Christian family, that the Church and the family may be said to constitute together one and the same temple of Christian education.

The School

77. Since, however, the younger generations must be trained in the arts and sciences for the advantage and prosperity of civil society, and since the family of itself is unequal to this task, it was necessary to create that social institution, the school. But let it be borne in mind that this institution owes its existence to the initiative of the family and of the Church, long before it was undertaken by the State. Hence, considered in its historical origin, the school is by its

very nature an institution subsidiary and complementary to the family and to the Church. It follows logically and necessarily that it must not be in opposition to, but in positive accord with those other two elements, and form with them a perfect moral union, constituting one sanctuary of education, as it were, with the family and the Church. Otherwise, it is doomed to fail of its purpose, and to become instead an agent of destruction.

78. This principle we find recognized by a layman, famous for his pedagogical writings, though these, because of their liberalism, cannot be unreservedly praised. "The school," he writes, "if not a temple, is a den." And again: "When literary, social, domestic, and religious education do not go hand in hand, man is unhappy and helpless."[185]

79. From this it follows that the so-called "neutral" or "lay" school, from which religion is excluded, is contrary to the fundamental principles of education. Such a school, moreover, cannot exist in practice; it is bound to become irreligious. There is no need to repeat what Our predecessors have declared on this point, especially Pius IX and Leo XIII, at times when laicism was beginning in a special manner to infest the public school. We renew and confirm their declarations,[186] as well as the sacred canons in which the frequenting of non-Catholic schools, whether neutral or mixed—those, namely, which are open to Catholics and non-Catholics alike—is forbidden for Catholic children, and can be at most tolerated, on the approval of the ordinary alone, under determined circum-

[185] Niccolò Tommaseo, *Pensieri sull' educazione* (Milan, 1864), pt. 1, chaps. 3, 6.

[186] See Pope Pius IX, *Quum non sine*; Syllabus of Errors (issued together with his Encyclical *Quanta cura*, [December 8, 1864]), prop. 48; Pope Leo XIII, Allocution *Summi Pontificatus* (August 20, 1880), in ASS, 13:49–55; *Nobilissima Gallorum*; Encyclical *Quod multum* (August 22, 1886); Encyclical *Officio sanctissimo* (December 22, 1887); Encyclical *Caritatis providentiaeque* (March 19, 1894); etc. See also *Code of Canon Law* [1917], can. 1374.

stances of place and time, and with special precautions.[187] Neither can Catholics admit that other type of mixed school, (least of all if it is the "only" one and all children are required to attend it), in which the students are provided with separate religious instruction, but receive other lessons in common with non-Catholic pupils from non-Catholic teachers.

The Catholic School

80. For the mere fact that a school gives some religious instruction (often extremely stinted), does not bring it into accord with the rights of the Church and of the Christian family, or make it a fit place for Catholic students. To be this, it is necessary that all the teaching and the whole organization of the school, and its teachers, syllabus, and textbooks in every branch, be regulated by the Christian spirit, under the direction and maternal supervision of the Church; so that religion may be in very truth the foundation and crown of the youth's entire training; and this in every grade of school, not only the elementary, but the intermediate and the higher institutions of learning as well. To use the words of Leo XIII:

> It is necessary not only that religious instruction be given to the young at certain fixed times, but also that every other subject taught be permeated with Christian piety. If this is wanting, if this sacred atmosphere does not pervade and warm the hearts of masters and scholars alike, little good can be expected from any kind of learning, and considerable harm will often be the consequence.[188]

81. And let no one say that in a nation where there are different religious beliefs, it is impossible to provide for public instruction otherwise than by neutral or mixed schools. In such a case it becomes the duty of the State, indeed it is the easier and more reasonable method of procedure, to leave free scope to the initiative of the

[187] See *Code of Canon Law* [1917], can. 1374.
[188] Encyclical *Militantis Ecclesiae* (August 1, 1897), no. 18.

Church and the family, while giving them such assistance as justice demands. That this can be done to the full satisfaction of families, and to the advantage of education and of public peace and tranquility, is clear from the actual experience of some countries comprising different religious denominations. There the school legislation respects the rights of the family, and Catholics are free to follow their own system of teaching in schools that are entirely Catholic. Nor is distributive justice lost sight of, as is evidenced by the financial aid granted by the State to the several schools demanded by the families.

82. In other countries of mixed creeds, things are otherwise, and a heavy burden weighs upon Catholics, who, under the guidance of their bishops and with the indefatigable cooperation of the clergy, secular and regular, support Catholic schools for their children entirely at their own expense; to this they feel obliged in conscience, and with a generosity and constancy worthy of all praise, they are firmly determined to make adequate provision for what they openly profess as their motto: "Catholic education in Catholic schools for all the Catholic youth." If such education is not aided from public funds, as distributive justice requires, certainly it may not be opposed by any civil authority ready to recognize the rights of the family, and the irreducible claims of legitimate liberty.

83. Where this fundamental liberty is thwarted or interfered with, Catholics will never feel, whatever may have been the sacrifices already made, that they have done enough, for the support and defense of their schools and for the securing of laws that will do them justice.

Catholic Action

84. For whatever Catholics do in promoting and defending the Catholic school for their children, is a genuinely religious work and there-

fore an important task of "Catholic Action." For this reason, the associations which in various countries are so zealously engaged in this work of prime necessity, are especially dear to Our paternal heart and are deserving of every commendation.

85. Let it be loudly proclaimed and well understood and recognized by all, that Catholics, no matter what their nationality, in agitating for Catholic schools for their children, are not mixing in party politics, but are engaged in a religious enterprise demanded by conscience. They do not intend to separate their children either from the body of the nation or its spirit, but to educate them in a perfect manner, most conducive to the prosperity of the nation. Indeed, a good Catholic, precisely because of his Catholic principles, makes the better citizen, attached to his country, and loyally submissive to constituted civil authority in every legitimate form of government.

86. In such a school, in harmony with the Church and the Christian family, the various branches of secular learning will not enter into conflict with religious instruction to the manifest detriment of education. And if, when occasion arises, it be deemed necessary to have the students read authors propounding false doctrine, for the purpose of refuting it, this will be done after due preparation and with such an antidote of sound doctrine, that it will not only do no harm, but will be an aid to the Christian formation of youth.

87. In such a school, moreover, the study of the vernacular and of classical literature will do no damage to moral virtue. There the Christian teacher will imitate the bee, which takes the choicest part of the flower and leaves the rest, as St. Basil teaches in his discourse to youths on the study of the classics.[189] Nor will this necessary caution, suggested also by the pagan Quintilian,[190] in any way hin-

[189] In *Patrologia Graeca*, t. 31, 570.

[190] See *Institutio Oratoria*, bk. 1, chap. 8.

der the Christian teacher from gathering and turning to profit, whatever there is of real worth in the systems and methods of our modern times, mindful of the apostle's advice: "Prove all things: hold fast that which is good" (1 Thes 5:21). Hence in accepting the new, he will not hastily abandon the old, which the experience of centuries has found expedient and profitable. This is particularly true in the teaching of Latin, which in our days is falling more and more into disuse, because of the unreasonable rejection of methods so successfully used by that sane humanism, whose highest development was reached in the schools of the Church. These noble traditions of the past require that the youth committed to Catholic schools be fully instructed in the letters and sciences in accordance with the exigencies of the times. They also demand that the doctrine imparted be deep and solid, especially in sound philosophy, avoiding the muddled superficiality of those "who perhaps would have found the necessary, had they not gone in search of the superfluous."[191] In this connection, Christian teachers should keep in mind what Leo XIII says in a pithy sentence: "Greater stress must be laid on the employment of apt and solid methods of teaching, and, what is still more important, on bringing into full conformity with the Catholic Faith, what is taught in literature, in the sciences, and above all in philosophy, on which depends in great part the right orientation of the other branches of knowledge."[192]

Good Teachers

88. Perfect schools are the result not so much of good methods as of good teachers, teachers who are thoroughly prepared and well-grounded in the matter they have to teach; who possess the intellectual and moral qualifications required by their important office; who cherish a pure and holy love for the youths confided to them, because they love Jesus Christ and His Church, of which these are

[191] Seneca, *Ep.* 45.

[192] Encyclical *Inscrutabili Dei consilio* (April 21, 1878), no. 13.

the children of predilection; and who have therefore sincerely at heart the true good of family and country. Indeed, it fills Our soul with consolation and gratitude toward the divine Goodness to see, side by side with religious men and women engaged in teaching, such a large number of excellent lay teachers, who, for their greater spiritual advancement, are often grouped in special sodalities and associations, which are worthy of praise and encouragement as most excellent and powerful auxiliaries of "Catholic Action." All these labor unselfishly with zeal and perseverance in what St. Gregory Nazianzen calls "the art of arts and the science of sciences,"[193] the direction and formation of youth. Of them also it may be said in the words of the divine Master: "The harvest indeed is great, but the laborers few" (Mt 9:37). Let us then pray the Lord of the harvest to send more such workers into the field of Christian education; and let their formation be one of the principal concerns of the pastors of souls and of the superiors of religious orders.

89. It is no less necessary to direct and watch the education of the adolescent, "soft as wax to be molded into vice,"[194] in whatever other environment he may happen to be, removing occasions of evil and providing occasions for good in his recreations and social intercourse; for "evil communications corrupt good manners" (1 Cor 15:33).

The World and Its Dangers

90. More than ever nowadays an extended and careful vigilance is necessary, inasmuch as the dangers of moral and religious shipwreck are greater for inexperienced youth. Especially is this true of impious and immoral books, often diabolically circulated at low prices; of the cinema, which multiplies every kind of exhibition; and now also of the radio, which facilitates every kind of communications. These most powerful means of publicity, which can be of great util-

[193] *Orat.* 2, no. 16.

[194] Horatius Flaccus, *De Arte Poetica liber*, v. 163.

ity for instruction and education when directed by sound principles, are only too often used as an incentive to evil passions and greed for gain. St. Augustine deplored the passion for the shows of the circus which possessed even some Christians of his time, and he dramatically narrates the infatuation for them, fortunately only temporary, of his disciple and friend Alipius.[195] How often today must parents and educators bewail the corruption of youth brought about by the modern theater and the vile book!

91. Worthy of all praise and encouragement therefore are those educational associations which have for their object to point out to parents and educators, by means of suitable books and periodicals, the dangers to morals and religion that are often cunningly disguised in books and theatrical representations. In their spirit of zeal for the souls of the young, they endeavor at the same time to circulate good literature and to promote plays that are really instructive, going so far as to put up at the cost of great sacrifices theaters and cinemas, in which virtue will have nothing to suffer and much to gain.

92. This necessary vigilance does not demand that young people be removed from the society in which they must live and save their souls; but that today more than ever they should be forewarned and forearmed as Christians against the seductions and the errors of the world, which, as Holy Writ admonishes us, is all "concupiscence of the flesh, concupiscence of the eyes, and pride of life" (1 Jn 2:16). Let them be what Tertullian wrote of the first Christians, and what Christians of all times ought to be, "sharers in the possession of the world, not of its error."[196]

[195] See *Confessionum*, bk. 6, chap. 8.
[196] *De idololatria*, chap. 14.

93. This saying of Tertullian brings us to the topic which we propose to treat in the last place, and which is of the greatest importance, that is, the true nature of Christian education, as deduced from its proper end. Its consideration reveals with noonday clearness the preeminent educational mission of the Church.

94. The proper and immediate end of Christian education is to cooperate with divine grace in forming the true and perfect Christian, that is, to form Christ Himself in those regenerated by baptism, according to the emphatic expression of the apostle: "My little children, of whom I am in labor again, until Christ be formed in you" (Gal 4:19). For the true Christian must live a supernatural life in Christ, "Christ, Who is your life" (Col 3:4), and display it in all his actions: "That the life also of Jesus may be made manifest in our mortal flesh" (2 Cor 4:11).

95. For precisely this reason, Christian education takes in the whole aggregate of human life, physical and spiritual, intellectual and moral, individual, domestic, and social, not with a view of reducing it in any way, but in order to elevate, regulate, and perfect it, in accordance with the example and teaching of Christ.

The True Christian

96. Hence the true Christian, product of Christian education, is the supernatural man who thinks, judges, and acts constantly and consistently in accordance with right reason, illumined by the supernatural light of the example and teaching of Christ; in other words, to use the current term, the true and finished man of character. For, it is not every kind of consistency and firmness of conduct based on subjective principles that makes true character, but only constancy in following the eternal principles of justice, as is admitted even by the pagan poet when he praises as one and the same "the

man who is just and firm of purpose."[197] And on the other hand, there cannot be full justice except in giving to God what is due to God, as the true Christian does.

97. The scope and aim of Christian education as here described appears to the worldly as an abstraction, or rather as something that cannot be attained without the suppression or dwarfing of the natural faculties, and without a renunciation of the activities of the present life, and hence inimical to social life and temporal prosperity, and contrary to all progress in letters, arts, and sciences, and all the other elements of civilization. To a like objection raised by the ignorance and the prejudice of even cultured pagans of a former day, and repeated with greater frequency and insistence in modern times, Tertullian has replied as follows:

> We are not strangers to life. We are fully aware of the gratitude we owe to God, Our Lord and Creator. We reject none of the fruits of His handiwork; we only abstain from their immoderate or unlawful use. We are living in the world with you; we do not shun your forum, your markets, your baths, your shops, your factories, your stables, your places of business and traffic. We take shop with you and we serve in your armies; we are farmers and merchants with you; we interchange skilled labor and display our works in public for your service. How we can seem unprofitable to you with whom we live and of whom we are, I know not.[198]

98. The true Christian does not renounce the activities of this life, he does not stunt his natural faculties; but he develops and perfects them, by coordinating them with the supernatural. He thus ennobles what is merely natural in life and secures for it new strength in the material and temporal order, no less, then, in the spiritual and eternal.

[197] Horatius Flaccus, *Carmina*, bk. 3, poem 3, v. 1.
[198] *Apologeticum*, chap. 42.

Evidence of History

99. This fact is proved by the whole history of Christianity and its institutions, which is nothing else but the history of true civilization and progress up to the present day. It stands out conspicuously in the lives of the numerous saints, whom the Church, and she alone, produces, in whom is perfectly realized the purpose of Christian education, and who have in every way ennobled and benefited human society. Indeed, the saints have ever been, are, and ever will be the greatest benefactors of society, and perfect models for every class and profession, for every state and condition of life, from the simple and uncultured peasant to the master of sciences and letters, from the humble artisan to the commander of armies, from the father of a family to the ruler of peoples and nations, from simple maidens and matrons of the domestic hearth to queens and empresses. What shall we say of the immense work which has been accomplished even for the temporal well-being of men by missionaries of the gospel, who have brought and still bring to barbarous tribes the benefits of civilization together with the light of the Faith? What of the founders of so many social and charitable institutions, of the vast numbers of saintly educators, men and women, who have perpetuated and multiplied their lifework, by leaving after them prolific institutions of Christian education, in aid of families and for the inestimable advantage of nations?

100. Such are the fruits of Christian education. Their price and value is derived from the supernatural virtue and life in Christ which Christian education forms and develops in man. Of this life and virtue Christ Our Lord and Master is the source and dispenser. By His example He is at the same time the universal model accessible to all, especially to the young in the period of His hidden life, a life of labor and obedience, adorned with all virtues, personal, domestic, and social, before God and men.

101. Now all this array of priceless educational treasures, which We have barely touched upon, is so truly a property of the Church as to form her very substance, since she is the Mystical Body of Christ, the immaculate Spouse of Christ, and consequently a most admirable mother and an incomparable and perfect teacher. This thought inspired St. Augustine, the great genius of whose blessed death we are about to celebrate the fifteenth centenary, with accents of tenderest love for so glorious a mother:

> O Catholic Church, true Mother of Christians! Not only doest thou preach to us, as is meet, how purely and chastely we are to worship God Himself, Whom to possess is life most blessed; thou doest, moreover, so cherish neighborly love and charity, that all the infirmities to which sinful souls are subject find their most potent remedy in thee. Childlike thou are in molding the child, strong with the young man, gentle with the aged, dealing with each according to his needs of mind and body. Thou doest subject child to parent in a sort of free servitude, and settest parent over child in a jurisdiction of love. Thou bindest brethren to brethren by the bond of religion, stronger and closer than the bond of blood.... Thou unitest citizen to citizen, nation to nation, yea, all men, in a union not of companionship only, but of brotherhood, reminding them of their common origin. Thou teachest kings to care for their people, and biddest people to be subject to their kings. Thou teachest assiduously to whom honor is due, to whom love, to whom reverence, to whom fear, to whom comfort, to whom rebuke, to whom punishment; showing us that whilst not all things nor the same things are due to all, charity is due to all and offense to none.[199]

102. Let us then, Venerable Brethren, raise our hands and our hearts in supplication to heaven, "to the Shepherd and Bishop of our souls" (1 Pt 2:25), to the divine King "Who gives laws to rulers," that in His almighty power He may cause these splendid fruits of Christian

[199] *De moribus Ecclesiae catholicae*, chap. 30, nos. 62–63.

education to be gathered in ever greater abundance "in the whole world," for the lasting benefit of individuals and of nations.

As a pledge of these heavenly favors, with paternal affection We impart to you, Venerable Brethren, to your clergy and your people, the Apostolic Benediction.

Given at Rome, at St. Peter's, the thirty-first day of December, in the year 1929, the eighth of Our Pontificate.

Provido Sane Consilium

DECREE OF THE SACRED CONGREGATION OF THE COUNCIL ON THE PROMOTION OF CATECHETICAL INSTRUCTION[200]

Pope Pius XI

January 12, 1935

1. Impelled by a truly provident counsel and with a view to discharging her most sacred office and duty of custodian and teacher of divinely revealed truth, the Catholic Church has from the beginning regarded it as one of her bounden duties to transmit catechetically, through the medium and ministry of legitimate teachers, the heavenly wisdom necessary for salvation to those who are to be initiated into Christ Our Lord and trained in His discipline—especially to the children and to those who are poorly instructed.

2. Herein the Church has acted prudently. For since the knowledge of every Christian is comprised in our divine Savior's saying, "This is eternal life, that they may know Thee, the only true God, and Jesus Christ Whom Thou hast sent" (Jn 17:3), this knowledge is rightly and properly comprehended in catechetical instruction, through which a summary of our knowledge of God and of Jesus Christ and His doctrine is proposed and explained to hearers, according to the age, mental capacity, and condition of life of each. When this knowledge is transmitted and explained, the faithful can scarcely desire any more suitable basis for attaining a sure and firm norm of correct belief and correct conduct.

[200] In AAS, 27:145–154.

"Let the Little Children Come to Me"

3. Hence, catechetical instruction has been and is regarded in the Catholic Church as that voice with which divine Wisdom keeps crying out in the streets: "If any one is little, let him come to Me" (Prv 9:4); as that lamp "shining in a misty place until the daystar shall rise" (2 Pt 1:19); as that evangelical "seed" or "leaven," wherefrom all Christian life germinates and wherewith it is fostered: having derived from this source the light of divine truth, the norm of the divine law, and the aids of divine grace, each member of the faithful may see what should be done, and acquire the strength to fulfill what he has seen. While indeed of great utility to all, this religious instruction is certainly most beneficial in the case of children and adolescents, since in them is vested the hope of the coming age. Consequently, the catechetical instruction of children and adolescents must be primarily provided for and emphasized, especially in an age when the secular education of children and adolescents is anticipated and pushed forward because of the more widely diffused zeal for knowledge, the multiplied facilities of learning, and the more suitable curricula: for it is absurd, in the face of such a display of subjects and such ardor for learning, to neglect or disregard the knowledge of God and of the most important things which are contained in religion.

4. It is evident that in the Catholic training and instruction of children and adolescents the safety of the State is also involved. For it is to the greatest interest of State and religion alike that citizens, while learning the principles of merely human knowledge and civil education, shall at the same time imbibe the Christian spirit.

5. It may thus be clearly understood with what equal love and wisdom the Church, as mistress of Catholic truth and discipline, cries out urgently, assuming the role of Christ: "Suffer little children to come unto Me, and forbid them not: for of such is the Kingdom of God" (Mk 10:14).

Concern of the Holy See

6. Having formed a correct judgment and conviction on all these matters, the Roman Pontiffs, the supreme teachers and leaders of the Catholic Faith, have never relaxed in their vigilance and diligence therein.

7. Passing over earlier instances, a most excellent testimony of this in recent days may be found in the Encyclical *Acerbo nimis* of Pope Pius X of April 15, 1905, in which this most vigilant pontiff, having described the advantages of catechetics (advantages which it shares with no other discipline), rightly concludes that the sole reason why faith is languishing and almost moribund in our age is because the office of transmitting Christian doctrine is being either discharged negligently or ignored. He therefore enacted laws governing the teaching of this doctrine to boys and girls, to adolescents, and finally to those advanced in years.

8. These laws, drafted into canons, are contained in the *Code of Canon Law*, in which the whole discipline concerning catechetical instruction to be observed in the universal Church is proposed and ordained.[201]

9. For the supervision of the laws contained in the Code and for their enforcement when circumstances demand it, Pope Pius XI by his Motu proprio *Orbem catholicum* of June 29, 1923, instituted the Catechetical Office (*Officium catechisticum*) in this Sacred Congregation, whose duty it is to supervise and promote all catechetical activity in the Catholic Church.

10. These commands and exhortations of the Supreme Pontiffs were seconded by the solicitude of the bishops, who in plenary or provincial councils, in diocesan synods, or in diocesan or national catechetical congresses, strove to establish catechetical instruction on a more scientific basis.

[201] See bk. 3, tit. 20, chap. 1, cann. 1329–1336.

11. However, despite these initial steps so promisingly taken everywhere, it is clear from the reports of these same bishops that there are still many things which impair the vigor and effect of Christian instruction. Chiefly to be lamented indeed is the indifference of the parents, of whom many, ignorant themselves of divine things, attach little or no importance to the religious training of their children. This is certainly a grave situation, since, if the parents are negligent or hostile, there is scarcely any hope that their children will receive a religious education.

12. The situation becomes even graver when, as is the case in some countries, the right of the Church in connection with the Christian training of youth is, because of party contentions, challenged or denied. For, impelled by sloth or fickleness or the very pressure of circumstances, the parents neither resist the unjust laws nor display any care or solicitude for the catechetical instruction of their children.

13. In regions where Catholics live among non-Catholics, and do not hesitate to enter into mixed marriages with them, it commonly happens that the married couple themselves and their children drift into a contempt for divine things, or fall entirely away from the Faith.

14. To this is added the apathy of the children and adolescents, who, distracted by other cares and allured by games and physical exercises, or attracted especially on feast days to profane spectacles characterized not rarely by relaxed morals, neglect to attend the parochial catechetical instruction. Thus, from their very earliest years, begin, to be aggravated daily, that neglect and forgetfulness of divine things which we so deeply deplore.

15. This forgetfulness and neglect cause all the more damage to the Faith, because the world has been invaded by rapacious wolves who have no mercy on the sheep; pseudo-teachers have insinuated

themselves, who, infected by atheism or neo-ethnicism, and indulging in human fictions and aberrations, strive cunningly by their writings and activities to overthrow the Catholic faith in God, in Jesus Christ, and in the ministry of the Church. Besides these must be mentioned all those who, inflamed by a zeal for propagating ill-starred Protestantism, preach a species of Christian doctrine and piety. It is incredible how easily all these deceive persons who are ignorant of or little conversant with Christian doctrine, and even simple and unwary members of the faithful.

16. Whilst the bishops and other pastors of souls already combat these evils with the utmost solicitude, such obstacles do not relieve this Sacred Congregation of the duty of repeatedly inciting their diligence, nor do they exempt these pastors themselves from bestowing ever greater care to that upon which depends, as may be seen, the eternal salvation of the sheep committed to their charge.

Further Catechetical Regulations

17. Wherefore, it has seemed opportune to this Sacred Congregation to urge all concerned with new incentives, and to issue to them certain precepts and suggestions whose observance holds out the hope that catechetical instruction will show better progress in the future.

18. In the first place, then, let the bishops, in view of the most grave authority and office entrusted to them, add even greater efforts and industry to the care and diligence which they have hitherto been accustomed to devote to catechetics. Wherefore, in accordance with Canon 336, § 2, "let them see that the faithful, especially the children and the unlettered, are given the nourishment of Christian doctrine, and that in the schools the instruction of children and adolescents is conducted according to the principles of the Catholic religion." And since, according to the precept of Canon 1336, "the local ordinary has the right within his own diocese to regulate

everything pertaining to the instruction of the people in Christian doctrine," let each ordinary consider carefully in the presence of the Lord what additional provisions and precepts should be made in connection with this most holy and necessary work, by what method he may more easily attain and effect that which he desires, being prepared to punish if necessary the negligent and recalcitrant with the ecclesiastical penalites specified in Canons 1333, § 2, and 2182. To the diligent, let him hold out the prospect of reward, by announcing that in the conferring of parishes and other benefices he will attach chief weight and importance to the zeal and diligence displayed toward catechetical instruction.

19. Secondly, let the pastors and others having the care of souls always remember that catechetical instruction is the foundation of the whole Christian life, and that to the proper giving of this instruction must be directed all their plans, studies, and labors. Let them, therefore, observe integrally and put into effect the precepts of Canons 1330, 1331, and 1332, and especially in this matter let them become all things to all men so that they may win all for Christ, and prove themselves faithful ministers and dispensers of the mysteries of God, carefully considering who have need of milk or who of more solid nutriment. To each and all let them supply the nourishment of doctrines which will augment their spirit, so that Christians will not only not be ignorant of those things which pertain to religion, or hold these things merely as a hereditary tradition, but will know and grasp these things in such a way that they will prove fruitful to themselves and to others.

20. In this most holy ministry, in accordance with Canon 1333, § 1, "let the pastors employ the aid of clerics living within the territory of the parish, and also, if necessary, of devout laypersons, especially of those who are enrolled in the Confraternity of Christian Doctrine or some similar sodality erected in the parish." Let all such persons, whether on invitation or command, willingly—nay, most

gladly—lend their assistance in this matter, as becomes the joyful givers whom the Lord loves.

21. And if the local ordinary should request it, let not the collaboration of the religious (which Canon 1334 demands) be withheld in a work which is so salutary, so pleasing to God, and so necessary for the good of souls. When called upon, let these religious rejoice, nay, let them be eager for the call, so that in this part of the Lord's domain also, where the harvest is great but the laborers few, they may perform meritorious service for the salvation of souls.

22. Finally, let parents and those holding the place of parents, from whom in this matter efficacious help and support are to be expected and demanded, remember that Canon 1113 binds them "by a most serious obligation to provide to the best of their ability for the religious and moral, no less than for the physical and civil, education of their children." And, according to Canon 1335, they must satisfy this obligation by seeing that their children receive catechetical instruction, and, according to Canon 1372, § 2, by providing for their Christian education.

23. All these things which we have thus summarized are indeed well known and understood, but let us not forget the proverb, *Repetita juvant*, especially since the matter in question is one on which enough can never be said.

Specific Commands for the Catechetical Apostolate

24. In order that the foregoing precepts may be more easily put into effect throughout the whole world, this Sacred Congregation, with the approval of His Holiness Pius XI, commands that the following regulations be executed in all dioceses:

25. 1. In every parish, besides the Confraternity of the Blessed Sacrament, there shall be instituted—and before all others—in accordance with Canon 711, § 2, a Confraternity of Christian Doctrine, embracing in its membership all who are capable of teaching or promoting catechetical instruction, especially schoolteachers and those who are experienced in the training of children.

26. 2. In every parish also, in accordance with the circular letter of this same Sacred Congregation to the ordinaries of Italy of April 23, 1924,[202] parochial catechetical schools shall be established where not already existing, in which, under the direction of the pastor and according to the method prescribed, children and adolescents will be taught the rudiments of the divine law and faith. To overcome the abovementioned grave indifference of parents, who think that their children are not bound to attend the parochial catechism class because religious instruction is given at home or in the public schools, the following regulations shall be observed diligently:

27. a) in accordance with the precept of Canon 1330, the pastors shall not admit to the due reception of the sacraments of penance and confirmation children who have not obtained the proper catechetical instruction according to the norm laid down in the Decree of the Sacred Congregation of the Sacraments of August 8, 1910;[203] and after children have received their First Communion, let the pastors labor to give them a more perfect and abundant knowledge of the catechism;

28. b) the pastors, preachers, confessors, and rectors of churches shall be insistent in warning especially the parents of the grave obligation by which they are bound to see "that all persons subject to them or entrusted to their care shall receive catechetical instruc-

[202] In AAS, 16:287–289.
[203] *Quam singulari*, in AAS, 2:577–583.

tion."[204] Pertinently, Benedict XIV declares in his Encyclical *Etsi minime* of February 7, 1742, no. 7: "It is also clear that the bishop himself may and should recommend most diligently to sacred orators that in their sermons they should impress on the ears and minds of parents that it is their concern to imbue their offspring with the mysteries of our religion; and if they are not qualified for this task, their children should be brought to church, where the precepts of the divine law are explained";

29. c) furthermore, let the pastors and other clergy strive their utmost to induce the children to attend the parochial catechism class with alert minds, employing for this purpose whatever means seem most appropriate—e.g., by celebrating a Mass for the children on the individual days of obligation, by announcing catechetical contests with prizes, by providing with moderation wholesome amusements and activities;

30. d) finally, let the pastors sedulously take care that, on the occasion of the pastoral visitations, the children shall prepare themselves to undergo an examination in the presence of the bishop, who shall seize this opportunity to make appropriate recommendations as to the points upon which he thinks the religious instruction in the parish is to be corrected, improved, and praised.

31. 3. But lest the religious instruction received in childhood should be forgotten with the advancement of age, and "since it has been found that not only adolescents and persons of riper years are in ignorance of divine things, but also adults and aged people are entirely inconversant with the salutary doctrine, either because they have never acquired it or because once acquired, it has gradually faded into oblivion,"[205] let the local ordinaries guard sedulously that the precept of Canon 1332 shall be observed sacredly by the

[204] *Code of Canon Law* [1917], can. 1335.
[205] Pope Benedict XIV, *Etsi minime*, no. 8.

pastors, by which the latter are bound "on Sundays and other feasts of obligation to give catechetical instructions to the adults in discourses adapted to their capacity." "In this connection," as Pius X commanded in his already mentioned Encyclical *Acerbo nimis*, "let them use the Catechism of the Council of Trent, and in such a sequence that, within an interval of four or five years, all the matter will be treated which deals with the Symbol, the sacraments, the Decalogue, prayer, and the precepts of the Church,"[206] as well as the evangelical counsels, grace, virtue, sin, and the last things.

32. Besides these precepts which must be observed by all, this same Sacred Congregation thinks it opportune to indicate to the local ordinaries some means which, as tested by experience, seem adapted to the desired end, so that each ordinary may introduce all or at least some of these means in his own diocese, as local needs and circumstances may suggest. Wherefore:

33. 1. As was provided for Italy in the letter of this Sacred Congregation of December 12, 1929, the local ordinaries shall institute, if possible, a Diocesan Catechetical Bureau (*Officium catechisticum*), which, under their direction, shall regulate all catechetical matters within the diocese. The chief duties of this bureau will be to see:

34. a) that in the parishes, schools, and colleges Christian doctrine shall be taught by qualified teachers according to the form handed down by the Church;

35. b) that, at fixed times, catechetical gatherings (*coetus catechistici*) and other conventions for schools of religion (which are discussed in the Decree of this Sacred Congregation of April 12, 1924)[207] shall be held to consider better means of promoting catechetical instruction;

[206] No. 24.
[207] In AAS, 16:431.

36. c) that special courses of lectures on religion (*series lectionum de religione*) shall be appointed each year for the fuller and more perfect training of those who teach Christian doctrine both in the public and in the parochial schools.

37. 2. Let the ordinaries not fail to select each year priest visitors (*Sacerdotes visitatores*), who shall inspect all the religion schools in the diocese, and shall make an accurate report concerning the results, successes, and defects of the religious instruction given. Benedict XIV says pertinently: "It will also contribute very greatly to the instruction of the Christian people if visitors are chosen, of whom some shall pass through the city and some through the diocese sedulously inquiring into everything, so that the bishop may be informed concerning the merits of each pastor, and may decree either rewards or penalties."[208]

38. 3. But in order that the Christian people may occasionally direct their thoughts to religious instruction in a special manner, a Catechetical Day (*Dies catechistica*) shall be instituted in each individual parish (if such is not already customary), on which a feast of Christian Doctrine should be celebrated with the greatest possible solemnity. On this occasion:

39. a) the faithful shall be assembled in the parish church to receive the Holy Eucharist and to pray that more abundant fruits of Christian doctrine may be obtained;

40. b) a special sermon shall be preached to the people on the particular necessity of catechetical instruction, in which the parents especially shall be warned to give their children this instruction, and to send them to the parochial catechism class, remembering the divine precept: "And these words which I command thee this day, shall be in thy heart, and thou shalt tell them to thy children" (Dt 6:6–7);

[208] *Etsi minime*, no. 16.

41. c) books, booklets, leaflets, and similar suitable material shall be distributed among the people;

42. d) a collection shall be taken for the promotion of catechetical work.

43. 4. In places especially where the clergy are so few that they cannot satisfactorily discharge the office of teaching Christian doctrine, the ordinaries shall strive to provide qualified catechists of both sexes to assist the pastors and give religious instruction in the parochial and public schools and in the remote places of the parish. Among these catechists, first place shall be taken by those who have enrolled in associations of Catholic Action. These associations have already performed many laudable services in this connection, and some of them have with excellent judgment commanded in their statutes that special lectures on religion be given annually, which all members are bound to attend.

44. Nor should the members of other Catholic associations and sodalities neglect this duty, especially religious sodalities of either sex that are dedicated to the training of youth. In the abovementioned Motu proprio *Orbem catholicum*, His Holiness Pope Pius XI addressed these sodalities as follows: "We are greatly desirous that, in the principal houses of religious sodalities devoted to the training of youth, schools should be opened under the direction and guidance of the bishops for selected adolescents of the two sexes, who shall be trained by a suitable curriculum of studies, and, after their knowledge has been tested, these shall be duly pronounced qualified to obtain the office of teaching Christian doctrine and sacred and ecclesiastical history."[209] This aim will be attained if, in Catholic schools and colleges, religious instruction shall hold the principal place (as reason itself suggests and demands) among the

[209] No. 5.

subjects to be learned by children and adolescents, and if this instruction is given according to a suitable curriculum and method by priests who are skilled in teaching.

45. If these means and activities are supplied, if to this task, than which there is none more holy or necessary, all whose duty it is will energetically and perseveringly direct their attention, we may entertain the justified hope that the Christian people, constantly guarded from the onslaughts of error by a holy and uncorrupted doctrine, will stand forth as an acceptable pursuer of good works, and will attain those salutary effects which the Roman Pontiffs have repeatedly inaugurated for the salvation of souls. Finally, with the approval of His Holiness Pope Pius XI, this Sacred Congregation commands the universal bishops that every five years (modifying in this respect the abovementioned Motu proprio *Orbem catholicum*)[210] they shall present an accurate report to this same Sacred Congregation regarding catechetical instruction in their dioceses according to the questions which follow, and observing the order laid down in Canon 340, § 2, of the *Code of Canon Law* with regard to the report to be made by the bishops on the state of the dioceses committed to them.

Issued at Rome, on the feast of the
Holy Family of Nazareth, January 12, 1935.

[210] Cf. no. 6.

QUESTIONNAIRE REGARDING THE TEACHING OF CHRISTIAN DOCTRINE[211]

I. For Children

A. In the Parishes

1. What is the number of the children in the individual parishes, and how many of these attend catechetical instruction?

2. What diligence do the pastors display in the fulfillment of their task of giving the children religious instruction, and what pastors neglect this duty?

3. Have parochial schools been instituted in these same parishes? With what result, and what method do they follow in teaching Christian doctrine?

4. Do the priests and other clerics living within the territory of the parish assist the pastor in teaching Christian doctrine? In what way is this assistance given? Have any been negligent or recalcitrant?

5. Do the religious of both sexes assist the pastor in teaching catechism to the children? Have any shown themselves negligent or recalcitrant?

6. Has the Confraternity of Christian Doctrine been established in the separate parishes, and in what way does it cooperate with the pastor in teaching Christian doctrine to the children?

7. Do other societies of the laity, especially of Catholic Action, assist the pastor in this same duty?

[211] Accessed May 15, 2025 online at https://www.ewtn.com/catholicism/library/on-better-care-for-catechetical-teaching-1981.

8. Has a Catechetical Bureau (*Officium catechisticum*) or some similar institute been established in the diocese, or is it possible to establish such?

9. Is a Catechetical Day celebrated? In what manner?

10. Are catechetical gatherings (*coetus catechistici*) held? With what fruits? Are other conventions for religion schools held?

11. Are any means employed to stimulate both parents and children, so that the latter will attend the parish catechism class? What means are employed?

12. Is there anything that interferes with the more abundant fruits of the teaching of Christian doctrine? What abuses have crept in, and what means are being employed, or may be employed, to remove them?

B. In Catholic Schools and Colleges

13. How many Catholic schools for boys and girls, especially of recent institution, are under the direction of the secular or regular clergy or of religious sisters?

14. How many pupils are there, day and boarders, in the individual Catholic schools and colleges?

15. How often during the week, and by what method and with what results, is religious instruction given in these schools?

16. How could this instruction be more efficaciously and usefully promoted?

C. In the Public Schools

17. Is Christian doctrine being taught in the public schools? In what schools, and with what success?

18. Is the religious instruction subject to the authority and inspection of the Church? In what way and in what public schools?

19. In what public schools, and for what reason, is Christian doctrine not taught? How is the religious instruction of the pupils of these schools being provided for?

20. Are any means employed, or can there be, to secure that Christian doctrine may be taught in these schools?

II. Adults

21. Besides the usual homily, is any catechetical instruction being given by the pastor to adults? When is this instruction given?

22. With what diligence, by what method, and at what time do the pastors fulfill this duty?

23. Do the faithful attend religious instruction in the individual parishes, and with what results?

24. In view of the circumstances of the time and place, what means are considered most suitable for promoting the more fruitful religious instruction of adults?

Appendix: Call for Capable Catechists

ADDRESS TO THE NATIONAL CATECHETICAL CONGRESS BY AMLETO GIOVANNI CARDINAL CICOGNANI, NEW YORK (OCTOBER 6, 1936)

"All who are capable should teach and foster the catechism."

1. One of the purposes of this National Catechetical Congress, and without doubt extremely important amongst its aims, is the desire to increase the number of those who work for the gospel of Christ in the teaching of catechism. "Going teach ye all nations" (Mt 28:19); "Go ye into the whole world, and preach the gospel to every creature" (Mk 16:15). This is the mandate given by Christ to His apostles, to His bishops: and on them rests the responsibility for religious teaching.

A General Invitation

2. Nevertheless, the honor of participating in that labor, of cooperating with it, of aiding and assisting it, particularly in the form of catechetical instruction, has been extensively and repeatedly offered to the faithful men and women of every age and of every condition of life. Only a little more than a year ago the latest fervent appeal of the Church for such cooperation was spoken in the Decree *Provido sane consilio* issued by the Sacred Congregation of the Council on January 12, 1935: "In places where on account of the scarcity of priests the clergy themselves cannot sufficiently perform the work of teaching Christian doctrine, let the bishops take active steps to supply capable catechists of both sexes to help the pastors. Let them teach religion in the parochial or in the public school, even

in the most remote parts of the parish."[212] The *Code of Canon Law* had previously commanded that, where needed, efforts should be encouraged on the part of "devout laypeople, especially those who have been enrolled in the Confraternity of Christian Doctrine."[213] Now, the new decree of the Holy See makes us understand that there should be associated together in this confraternity *omnes quot sunt idonei catechismo edocendo et fovendo*—"all who are capable of teaching and enkindling love for the catechism."[214] It is an urgent appeal, and today the National Catechetical Congress sounds it forth again to American Catholics.

3. There is no question here of an instruction in which the truths of faith are to be expounded with learned comments or scientific study, with philosophic proofs or controversial arguments. We are thinking only of a simple colloquy between teacher and pupil. We are considering an echo, as the derivation of the word *catechism* indicates—the echo of those clear and plain assertions of the divine Master which are spoken for the instruction and edification of those who desire to hear the Word of God.

4. St. Paul, writing to the Corinthians, sets forth a beautiful concept of catechetical instruction. The apostle and teacher of the Gentiles had received a special privilege from God of mastering languages, the charisma known as the gift of tongues. He did not neglect it. Rather, he declared: "I thank my God I speak with all your tongues" (1 Cor 14:18). But he went on to add that in the assemblage of the faithful he preferred to speak five words in his own way—that is, adapting them to the conditions of those who would hear them, that they might understand them and be instructed by them—rather than to speak ten thousand words with his gift of tongues, when the people might not understand.

[212] No. 43.
[213] Can. 1333.
[214] Sacred Congregation of the Council, *Provido sane consilio*, no. 25.

5. The ideal instruction, therefore, does not point out many things nor insist on what is extraordinary. Instead, it dwells upon a few sound principles, those which give direction to life and guide our steps along the pathways of righteousness. With this simple method, the Church has changed the customs of whole nations and of great peoples. With it, she has given education and formation to youth, and, with it, she conducts her missions and carries on her work today. Thousands of women have dedicated themselves in our Sisterhoods to forming Christ in the souls of children. How much of good they have done is ignored by the world! They deserve our deepest gratitude. Under the direction of the Church, many orders and religious institutes have risen with the chief task of teaching the catechism, as, for example, those of St. Jerome Aemilian, St. Philip Neri, St. Joseph Calasanctius, and St. John Baptist de la Salle. The Church has encouraged the drawing up in writing of catechetical instruction ever since the earliest ages of Christian history, and more especially since the Council of Trent and the marvelous work done by St. Peter Canisius, St. Robert Bellarmine, and many others.[215] It was on October 6, 1571, that the Sovereign Pontiff St. Pius V gave approval at Rome of the Confraternity of Christian Doctrine; and now it is the law of the Church that this confraternity be established in every parish.[216]

THE VALUE OF THE CATECHISM

6. The catechism is a small book, but it sets forth the gospel in brief formulas which can be readily understood. Through the catechism, children of every age in the history of the Church have become strong in faith, sincere and veritable theologians. From it the young have received a formative influence in every field of activity and in every social environment. It is a tiny book, but it is the fountan-

[215] Editor's Note: For a collection of the most outstanding traditional catechisms, see *Tradivox Catholic Catechism Index*, ed. Aaron Seng (Sophia Institute Press, 2020–2025).

[216] See *Code of Canon Law* [1917], can. 711, § 2.

head of the universal science which touches upon all divine and human knowledge. It is a true fountain of life in the fullest sense of the word, pouring forth rivers of living water in all directions.

7. In the terrible trials with which countries are now afflicted, their rulers are trying anxiously every remedy proposed for our great social evils. More than anything else, the nations have need of God. There is urgent and supreme need for the truths of faith. Souls have need of life; and the soul is truly and fully alive when it keeps up contact with God; when it recognizes Him as the Author and Creator of life; when it knows that the eternal Word became man to be our Master, Redeemer, and Savior; when it receives the gifts of the Holy Ghost and His grace; when it stands secure in the knowledge that the Church is the continuation of the Incarnation and of the teaching of Jesus Christ; when it exercises active membership in the Church Militant in piety and the reception of the sacraments, through which true peace of soul and sanctity of life are attained; when it looks with firm hope to life eternal and lays up for itself not treasures of this earth but of heaven. These are the contents of the catechism, a compendium of divine revelation.

The Greatest Evil of Our Time

8. To have forgotten or neglected these things, or perhaps never to have known them, is the greatest evil of our time. The Holy Pontiff Pope Pius X, in his Encyclical *Acerbo nimis* of April 15, 1905, making a diagnosis of the evils which afflict society, declared that the greatest misfortune and the greatest disaster was "ignorance of divine things."[217] In his zeal as supreme shepherd of souls, he pointed out to the bishops and parish priests that it is their first duty to instruct the people in religion. He commanded that everywhere the Confraternity of Christian Doctrine should be organized. He laid down rules for the teaching of catechism to children and adults,

[217] No. 1.

and he warmly recommended the selection of "able coworkers amongst devout laypeople to assist in this salutary work."[218]

9. Ignorance of the things of God is fatal both for the individual and for society. It tends naturally to intellectual and moral suicide. Human respect and the passions claim many victims; but ignorance has many more, because it takes away the light from our eyes, and blinds both the great and the lowly. Reason is a guide to faith, and the human mind is, as it were, naturally Christian; but with doubt and prejudice and indifference, this power is destroyed.

10. Visit the prisons and you will see that the greatest part of their unhappy inmates have neglected its lessons or never know their catechism at all. Enter into the families where there are moral disorders, and you will find lack of attention to the catechism. To save the world from many crimes and social maladies, to save many poor misguided souls from the misery of their state, the short lessons of the catechism would suffice. Where this instruction is lacking, it is easy to lead into evil ways those who are ignorant of the things of God, to bring about the acceptance of theories that are perverse and horrible, even to take man back to a state which borders on savagery. It is a fact that the most fertile field for the cultivation of wickedness is ignorance of the doctrines of Christ, and that irreligion and contempt for the things of God grow best in such a soil.

11. It is of supreme importance to the nations themselves that catechism be taught when human nature is the more genuine and sincere, and that mankind be given then the spiritual food which by nature it was designed to receive. Childhood is the strategic point of greatest importance in the life of man, and even more is this true when we consider the public weal and the advancement of civilization. It is in childhood, when the soul is a stranger to corruption,

[218] No. 22.

devoid of prejudice, and not yet seized upon by the artifices and deceits of the world, that the moral precepts and the postulates of virtue make us hear their voice the more readily. It is then that souls are more willing to tread the pathways of virtue, and conscience is more prompt to mold itself according to the dictates of eternal truth. But it is necessary that there be someone to set forth these truths of God and give these divine directions of life.

Who Should Heed This Appeal?

12. In the face of this extreme and compelling need, the Church places before our eyes a picture of the divine Savior going about through the cities and towns, teaching and preaching to the people: "And seeing the multitudes, He had compassion on them: because they were distressed, and lying like sheep that have no shepherd. Then He saith to His disciples: The harvest indeed is great, but the laborers are few. Pray ye, therefore, the Lord of the harvest, that He send forth laborers into His harvest" (Mt 9:36–38).

13. To every upright soul who lives the religion of Christ, it can well be said in the name of the selfsame Savior: "Go you also into My vineyard" (Mt 20:4). If you are united to God, and religion is the bond with God, you will readily understand the questions and answers of the catechism, and it will not be too difficult for you to repeat them to others and to impress them upon the minds and hearts of children.

Method of Teaching

14. Teaching the catechism is indeed directed to enlightenment of the mind, but substantially it is the purpose of Christian education to incline the will toward good and to direct the pupil toward a spiritual life and the acceptance of the sweet yoke of the divine Savior. The great masters of the catechism have been those who, expressing the truth in simplest fashion, have succeeded in conducting their stu-

dents to the practical application of their religious training in a life marked by the harmonious blending of knowledge and virtue.

15. A certain deacon at Carthage asked St. Augustine for practical directions in the teaching of Christian doctrine, and the holy Doctor answered him with a book entitled *De Catechizandis Rudibus*. There are applied in it the best principles of pedagogy and psychology: do not confound the young with too many facts, nor even the others who may be being catechized; do not tire the memory; insist on what is substantial or important, and omit the rest, or at least pass over it lightly; present the truth clearly and entirely, but adapt your presentation to the intelligence of your listeners, and with the slower ones make use of many comparisons and illustrations; put forward the love of God as your principal theme and central purpose; aim above all at purity of heart; proceed with that charity which made St. Paul write to the Galatians: "My little children, of whom I am in labor again, until Christ be formed in you" (Gal 4:19). These are not difficult rules. All who are animated by love of God and neighbor may well render themselves capable of teaching and enkindling love for the catechism if they take these suggestions to heart. It is not a passing philosophy the catechism contains, but the eternal truth, easy to impart if it is lived, and so easy to understand that the apostle compares it with milk, a material food which can be assimilated at any age.

We Must Live the Catechism

16. Our Holy Father Pope Pius XI has repeated many times that the catechism needs not only to be known but to be lived, and that we ought so to live it as to conform our whole life to its teaching. In fact, our lives reflect our viewpoints and our ideals. If these be harmful or godless, our lives will be godless and harmful. If our views are Christian, our life will be Christian. St. Paul could say, "To me, to live is Christ" (Phil 1:21), because his doctrine was that

of Christ. With the external work of the teacher, the inner working of grace will be in agreement, and, with faithfulness to grace, there cannot but be perseverance in godliness. Even with the passing years, good habits will be more firmly rooted, religious principles will extend their influence over every activity, and both the individual and human society will profit immensely.

Urgent Appeal

17. As many of you, therefore, as love Christ and His gospel, as many of you as are capable or can render yourselves capable of teaching and fostering the catechism, as many of you as love honesty, propriety, and uprightness of life, as many of you as are persuaded that the family is a sanctuary and that marriage is and ought to be a holy union whose sublime aim is the procreation and education of children—every one of you, therefore, take an interest in the teaching of catechism. As many of you as love your country, its laws, its prosperity, and its progress, as many of you as have at heart the interests of civilization—all of you, therefore, foster, sustain, and spread abroad the doctrine of Christ, help to carry it into every parish and mission, into every angle and corner of this great nation. Through these efforts, honesty, sobriety, and industry will be increased amongst the citizens of the land, the moral treasury of the nation will grow larger and larger, and you will secure for those whom you influence both choicest blessings here and eternal life hereafter.

SOPHIA INSTITUTE

Sophia Institute is a nonprofit institution that seeks to nurture the spiritual, moral, and cultural life of souls and to spread the Gospel of Christ in conformity with the authentic teachings of the Roman Catholic Church.

Sophia Institute Press fulfills this mission by offering translations, reprints, and new publications that afford readers a rich source of the enduring wisdom of mankind.

Sophia Institute also operates the popular online resource Catholic Exchange.com. *Catholic Exchange* provides world news from a Catholic perspective as well as daily devotionals and articles that will help readers to grow in holiness and live a life consistent with the teachings of the Church.

In 2013, Sophia Institute launched Sophia Institute for Teachers to renew and rebuild Catholic culture through service to Catholic education. With the goal of nurturing the spiritual, moral, and cultural life of souls, and an abiding respect for the role and work of teachers, we strive to provide materials and programs that are at once enlightening to the mind and ennobling to the heart; faithful and complete, as well as useful and practical.

Sophia Institute gratefully recognizes the Solidarity Association for preserving and encouraging the growth of our apostolate over the course of many years. Without their generous and timely support, this book would not be in your hands.

www.SophiaInstitute.com
www.CatholicExchange.com
www.SophiaTeachers.org

Sophia Institute Press® is a registered trademark of Sophia Institute.
Sophia Institute is a tax-exempt institution as defined by the Internal Revenue Code, Section 501(c)(3). Tax ID 22-2548708.